Addiction

OPPOSING VIEWPOINTS ®

OTHER BOOKS OF RELATED INTEREST

OPPOSING VIEWPOINTS SERIES

Alcohol
Chemical Dependency
Drug Abuse
Mental Health
Teens at Risk
Tobacco and Smoking
The War on Drugs

CURRENT CONTROVERSIES SERIES

Alcoholism
Gambling
Illegal Drugs
Mental Health
Smoking
Teen Addiction
Teen Smoking

AT ISSUE SERIES

Eating Disorders
Marijuana
Smoking

Addiction

OPPOSING VIEWPOINTS ®

Jennifer A. Hurley, *Book Editor*

David L. Bender, *Publisher*
Bruno Leone, *Executive Editor*
Bonnie Szumski, *Editorial Director*
David M. Haugen, *Managing Editor*

OPPOSING
VIEWPOINTS®
SERIES

Greenhaven Press, Inc., San Diego, California

Library of Congress Cataloging-in-Publication Data

Addiction : opposing viewpoints / Jennifer A. Hurley, book editor.
    p.   cm. — (Opposing viewpoints series)
    Includes bibliographical references and index.
    ISBN 0-7377-0116-1 (pbk. : alk. paper). —
ISBN 0-7377-0117-X (lib. : alk. paper)
    1. Drug abuse—United States. 2. Alcoholism—United States. 3. To-
bacco habit—United States. I. Hurley, Jennifer A., 1973– . II. Series:
Opposing viewpoints series (Unnumbered)
HV5825.A647 2000
362.29'0973—dc21
                                          99-10734
                                              CIP

Greenhaven Press, Inc., P.O. Box 289009
San Diego, CA 92198-9009

"CONGRESS SHALL MAKE NO LAW...ABRIDGING THE FREEDOM OF SPEECH, OR OF THE PRESS."

First Amendment to the U.S. Constitution

The basic foundation of our democracy is the First Amendment guarantee of freedom of expression. The Opposing Viewpoints Series is dedicated to the concept of this basic freedom and the idea that it is more important to practice it than to enshrine it.

CONTENTS

WHY CONSIDER OPPOSING VIEWPOINTS?

"The only way in which a human being can make some approach to knowing the whole of a subject is by hearing what can be said about it by persons of every variety of opinion and studying all modes in which it can be looked at by every character of mind. No wise man ever acquired his wisdom in any mode but this."

John Stuart Mill

In our media-intensive culture it is not difficult to find differing opinions. Thousands of newspapers and magazines and dozens of radio and television talk shows resound with differing points of view. The difficulty lies in deciding which opinion to agree with and which "experts" seem the most credible. The more inundated we become with differing opinions and claims, the more essential it is to hone critical reading and thinking skills to evaluate these ideas. Opposing Viewpoints books address this problem directly by presenting stimulating debates that can be used to enhance and teach these skills. The varied opinions contained in each book examine many different aspects of a single issue. While examining these conveniently edited opposing views, readers can develop critical thinking skills such as the ability to compare and contrast authors' credibility, facts, argumentation styles, use of persuasive techniques, and other stylistic tools. In short, the Opposing Viewpoints Series is an ideal way to attain the higher-level thinking and reading skills so essential in a culture of diverse and contradictory opinions.

In addition to providing a tool for critical thinking, Opposing Viewpoints books challenge readers to question their own strongly held opinions and assumptions. Most people form their opinions on the basis of upbringing, peer pressure, and personal, cultural, or professional bias. By reading carefully balanced opposing views, readers must directly confront new ideas as well as the opinions of those with whom they disagree. This is not to simplistically argue that everyone who reads opposing views will—or should—change his or her opinion. Instead, the series enhances readers' understanding of their own views by encouraging confrontation with opposing ideas. Careful examination of others' views can lead to the readers' understanding of the logical inconsistencies in their own opinions, perspective on why they hold an opinion, and the consideration of the possibility that their opinion requires further evaluation.

EVALUATING OTHER OPINIONS

To ensure that this type of examination occurs, Opposing Viewpoints books present all types of opinions. Prominent spokespeople on different sides of each issue as well as well-known professionals from many disciplines challenge the reader. An additional goal of the series is to provide a forum for other, less known, or even unpopular viewpoints. The opinion of an ordinary person who has had to make the decision to cut off life support from a terminally ill relative, for example, may be just as valuable and provide just as much insight as a medical ethicist's professional opinion. The editors have two additional purposes in including these less known views. One, the editors encourage readers to respect others' opinions—even when not enhanced by professional credibility. It is only by reading or listening to and objectively evaluating others' ideas that one can determine whether they are worthy of consideration. Two, the inclusion of such viewpoints encourages the important critical thinking skill of objectively evaluating an author's credentials and bias. This evaluation will illuminate an author's reasons for taking a particular stance on an issue and will aid in readers' evaluation of the author's ideas.

As series editors of the Opposing Viewpoints Series, it is our hope that these books will give readers a deeper understanding of the issues debated and an appreciation of the complexity of even seemingly simple issues when good and honest people disagree. This awareness is particularly important in a democratic society such as ours in which people enter into public debate to determine the common good. Those with whom one disagrees should not be regarded as enemies but rather as people whose views deserve careful examination and may shed light on one's own.

Thomas Jefferson once said that "difference of opinion leads to inquiry, and inquiry to truth." Jefferson, a broadly educated man, argued that "if a nation expects to be ignorant and free . . . it expects what never was and never will be." As individuals and as a nation, it is imperative that we consider the opinions of others and examine them with skill and discernment. The Opposing Viewpoints Series is intended to help readers achieve this goal.

David L. Bender & Bruno Leone,
Series Editors

Greenhaven Press anthologies primarily consist of previously published material taken from a variety of sources, including periodicals, books, scholarly journals, newspapers, government documents, and position papers from private and public organizations. These original sources are often edited for length and to ensure their accessibility for a young adult audience. The anthology editors also change the original titles of these works in order to clearly present the main thesis of each viewpoint and to explicitly indicate the opinion presented in the viewpoint. These alterations are made in consideration of both the reading and comprehension levels of a young adult audience. Every effort is made to ensure that Greenhaven Press accurately reflects the original intent of the authors included in this anthology.

INTRODUCTION

"Scientific research into addiction . . . has led experts to conclude that addiction is actually a disease, a chronic illness like diabetes or hypertension."
—Janet Firshein, independent health writer and former editor of Medicine and Health

"The disease concept [of addiction] is directly contradicted by a huge amount of research."
—Neal Williams, writer for Gray Areas, a magazine exploring controversial social issues

Throughout history, the prevailing attitude toward addiction has been one of disapproval, even repugnance. Addiction was seen as a personal failing, one that resulted from moral weakness and a lack of discipline. At best, addiction was a bad habit, at worst, a sin.

Although addiction has not entirely lost its stigma, an increasing body of scientific research has improved people's understanding of and sympathy for the problem. One major development in addiction research is the theory that addiction is primarily a biological phenomenon. As Alan I. Leshner, director of the National Institute on Drug Abuse, puts it, addiction is "literally a disease of the brain."

For years, addiction researchers have asserted that alcoholism has a genetic basis. According to John Crabbe, a researcher at Oregon Health Sciences University and the Veterans Affairs Medical Center, "Alcohol dependence in humans is clearly influenced by genes as well as environmental factors. There is clearly an increased risk for severe alcohol-related problems in children of alcoholics, . . . even if they have been raised without knowledge of their biological parents' problems." While studies seem to support the view that alcoholism is genetic, identifying the specific genes that lead to an increased risk of alcoholism has been a laborious task, since humans express more than one hundred thousand genes. However, in 1997, researchers at the Portland Alcohol Center announced that they had mapped three gene regions in mice that influence susceptibility to physical dependence on alcohol—information that they believe could lead to the development of new treatments for alcoholics.

Furthermore, research documenting the impact of drugs on the brain may shed light on why some people are more prone to addiction than others. Drug use—along with other potentially addictive activities such as gambling or sex—causes the brain to release dopamine, a chemical involved in experiencing pleasure. This surge in dopamine can be so powerful that it compels users to keep taking the drug. With prolonged use, however, drugs can alter the brain so that experiencing pleasure without the drug is nearly impossible. At this point, drug use does not raise dopamine levels or produce a "high"; instead, the user keeps taking the drug to stave off painful withdrawal symptoms such as fever, cramps, violent nausea, and depression.

Based on their research of how drugs affect the brain, scientists have theorized that people who are deficient in dopamine may be more likely than others to become addicts. George Koob, a professor of neuropharmacology at the Scripps Research Institute in La Jolla, California, contends that the neurotransmitter systems affected by drug abuse may already be abnormal in people who are susceptible to addiction.

But while most people agree that biology plays some role in addiction, experts on addiction are generally separated into two camps: those who believe that addiction is a biological disease with behavioral aspects, and those who believe that addiction is primarily a behavioral problem that is sometimes influenced by biology.

The latter group maintains that labeling addiction as a medical condition creates a false assumption that addicts have no control over their own behavior. In the view of this group, people become addicts because of their behavior, not their brain chemistry. Neal Williams, a critic of the notion that biology is responsible for addiction, says that "the disease concept is so popular [because] it gives people an easy way out. They believe that they inherited their addiction, therefore they're not responsible for their own behavior."

Other critics question whether scientific research has proven that addiction is biological. Stanton Peele, a vociferous opponent of the belief that addiction is a disease, contends that the disease model of addiction is flawed for a number of reasons. First, he claims, most people who take drugs do not become addicted, but may take drugs for a period of time, then stop when they choose to do so. For example, most smokers who successfully kick their addiction to nicotine—a drug purportedly more addictive than heroin—rely solely on willpower to do so. Second, Peele challenges the theory that dopamine is responsible for addiction. He states, "The wide range of activities that stimulate the pleasure centers of the brain—including sex, eating, working, chocolate—should alert us that these brain theories tell us nothing about differences in behavior, let alone addiction. . . . Chocolate stimulates the pleasure centers, but only a few people compulsively eat chocolate or sweets. Apparently, stimulation of the pleasure center is only one small component in the entire addiction syndrome."

The two contrasting perspectives on addiction—biological versus behavioral—influence debate over the appropriate way to treat drug addicts and alcoholics. Those who believe addiction is a disease generally favor a treatment plan that includes both counseling and medications. Moreover, they maintain that abstinence is the best way to break an addiction to drugs or alcohol. In contrast, opponents of the disease model insist that many addicts recover without any type of psychological or medical intervention—and that some are able to moderate their intake of drugs or alcohol. In the following chapters—What Factors Contribute to Addiction? Is Addiction a Serious Problem? How Should Addiction Be Treated? How Should the Government Deal with Addiction?—Addiction: Opposing Viewpoints provides a variety of perspectives on the nature of addiction, and offers opposing views on the treatments and policies proposed to control this troubling problem.

CHAPTER 1

WHAT FACTORS CONTRIBUTE TO ADDICTION?

CHAPTER PREFACE

With substance abuse considered by many to have reached epidemic proportions, researchers are attempting to identify the factors that make people susceptible to drug addiction. One theory that has emerged is the "gateway" hypothesis: the belief that the use of alcohol, tobacco products, or marijuana often leads to experimentation with harder drugs. Some analysts believe that marijuana users are extremely likely to use—and become hooked on—highly addictive and often debilitating drugs such as heroin and cocaine. The reasons offered for this phenomenon range from claims that marijuana use alters the chemistry of the brain, thereby "priming" it for other drugs, to the assertion that marijuana use introduces people to a subculture in which hard drugs are readily accessible.

The gateway hypothesis has been the basis for a government ad campaign that portrays marijuana as an extremely dangerous drug. But not everyone believes that this approach is wise. In fact, some critics contend that any gateway effect of marijuana can be eliminated by making the drug legal. A governmental report issued by the Netherlands, where marijuana (but not other drugs) can be legally purchased in small amounts, states that "there is no physically determined tendency toward switching from [marijuana] to harder substances. Social factors, however, do play a role. The more users become integrated in an environment ('subculture') where, apart from cannabis, hard drugs can also be obtained, the greater the chance that they may switch to hard drugs. Separation of the drug markets is therefore essential."

The belief that marijuana use fosters addiction is likely to remain controversial. In the chapter that follows, authors provide contrasting views on the question of what factors contribute to the problem of addiction.

| "Drug addiction, drug craving and relapse into drug use are not signs of psychological or moral weakness but rather the result of a powerful chain of molecular events."

ADDICTION IS A DISEASE

Eric Niiler

In the following viewpoint, Eric Niiler, staff writer for the *San Diego Union-Tribune*, contends that people are genetically predisposed to addiction—which is why some people can use drugs and alcohol recreationally, while others quickly become addicts. For some, drugs such as heroin, cocaine, and nicotine produce high levels of the brain chemical dopamine, which is associated with pleasure. The surge of dopamine produced by taking drugs is so powerful that addicts find quitting nearly impossible.

As you read, consider the following questions:

1. According to statistics provided by Niiler, what is the respective addictiveness of nicotine, heroin, cocaine, alcohol, amphetamines, and marijuana?
2. According to Niiler, what role does dopamine play in addiction?

Reprinted from Eric Niiler, "Hooked on a Feeling: Brain Researchers Unravel the Biochemistry of Addiction," *San Diego Union-Tribune*, May 27, 1998, page E-1, by permission of the *San Diego Union-Tribune*.

Not long ago, brain researcher George Koob was showing slides of experimental rats receiving cocaine to a group of medical workers at UCSD. During the presentation, a man in the front row began sweating, his face turning red. He began shaking in his seat.

The man—a physician—had kicked his cocaine habit three years earlier. But simply seeing images of lab rats set off an overwhelming physical urge to once again seek the drug.

"It was very powerful," said Koob, director of neuropharmacology at Scripps Research Institute. "He told me he was craving cocaine."

In the past decade, Koob and other researchers have learned that drug addiction, drug craving and relapse into drug use are not signs of psychological or moral weakness but rather the result of a powerful chain of molecular events that eventually compels an addict to get another fix, hit or drink.

This chain reaction affects some people more than others, leading scientists to believe that genetics are somehow involved in drug dependency. That's why, they believe, some people can use recreational drugs or alcohol and then stop, while others find themselves addicted after the first experience. Researchers such as Koob are exploring the molecular basis of drug addiction and its links to human behavior. They are gaining new insights into the brain's reward system—the "pleasure pathway"—and how it gets hijacked by addictive substances.

To do this, they are using sophisticated new computer imaging technology that lights up the brain like a pinball machine as the user experiences the high of drug use. At the same time, they are relying on old-fashioned experiments in which human observers watch as lab rats press levers in their cage to get rewarded with drug injections.

This flowering area of research has important implications for treating alcoholism, smoking and drug addiction. The collective national cost of these diseases in treatment, lost work time and deaths surpassed $256 billion in 1995, according to federal estimates, greater than that of cancer and heart disease combined.

Nicotine is the most addictive substance. About one-third of people who smoke become addicted. Heroin is addictive in about one-quarter of its users, followed by cocaine and alcohol at 16 and 15 percent, respectively; amphetamines at 11 percent; and marijuana at 9 percent, according to the National Institute of Medicine.

At the same time, hospital patients who are given morphine

don't become hooked on the drug once they have healed. The answer to this riddle of addiction lies in our brains.

"The time is right for making the full frontal attack on drug addiction," said Robert Malenka, director of the new Center for the Neurobiology of Addiction at UC San Francisco.

"It's been done for cancer, diabetes and heart disease. This is the first time that drug addiction, which has enormous stigma attached to it, has gotten the same attention. It's the first time we've acknowledged it as a disease."

PLEASURE'S REWARDS

The brain's pleasure pathway, known as the mesolimbic reward system, evolved to help us survive as a species. It makes us feel good when we eat, socialize or procreate.

The sensation is caused by the release of dopamine, a chemical messenger that links pleasure-regulating structures in the center of the brain to the higher areas behind the forehead that control conscious thought.

Dopamine is involved in all kinds of rewarded behavior, from parents nurturing their infants to the high felt during sex. It possibly even has a role in love. Dopamine keeps us doing things that are good for us in the long run.

The brain's ventral tegmental area is the source of dopamine, which travels to the nucleus accumbens, a tiny structure the size of a squished pea. A connected structure called the amygdala gets activated when human subjects take opiate drugs, such as heroin.

Scientists have known since the 1950s that the brain contains a pleasure center, but only recently have they been able to diagram the sequence of events along the neural pathway.

In 1995, researchers added nicotine to the list of dopamine-stimulating substances. Earlier this month, Koob's lab published findings in the British journal Nature that nicotine withdrawal disrupts the reward system and may force smokers to light up again after trying to quit.

During every-day pleasurable activities, like eating chocolate cake, dopamine levels rise in the brain before falling back to normal levels.

But when addicts take their drug of choice, it's as if someone opened up the dopamine floodgates and released up to 10 times more than would a bite of chocolate.

Drugs are carried by the bloodstream into the brain's dopamine pathway, where they stimulate surrounding brain cells and cause them to give off an electrical impulse that triggers nearby cells. The result is a massive production of dopamine.

The pleasure doesn't last very long, but in some people it creates a desire for more of the same. What researchers are finding out in laboratory studies is that the drug-taking physically changes the brain over time by decreasing the nerve endings that receive dopamine, called receptors.

Doctors have long known that it's harder for drug addicts to feel good when they don't have that extra boost of dopamine. That's because their brains have adapted to keep functioning while swamped in larger and larger amounts of drug-generated dopamine.

When the supply of the drug—whether it's nicotine, alcohol, cocaine, heroin or amphetamines—stops, the brain cries out for more. When addicts say they can't help themselves (ignoring their own personal safety, well being or relationships to obtain another rush), it's really their brain talking.

MIND-BODY CONNECTION

This connection between mind and body is clearly illuminated in images taken of drug addicts' brains. Using a positron emission tomography scanning (PET scan) device, researchers are now able to watch an individual's brain light up in color as the patient takes a drug.

Edythe London, a National Institute on Drug Abuse (NIDA) researcher, has performed these scans during patients' drug craving behavior. She's found that even the suggestion of drugs stimulates the brain's reward system. That's what was happening to the cocaine-craving doctor listening to Koob's lecture.

London, who outlined her work at a recent conference at UCSF, compared the brains of cocaine users who watched videos of nature programs to the same group as they watched videos of drug-taking, drug paraphernalia and places where drugs are used.

Brain metabolism skyrocketed in several regions when the cocaine videos were shown, but remained static during the nature shows.

The studies support the idea that drug addicts and alcoholics fare better during rehabilitation if they can get out of their surroundings.

Because the reward system is closely linked with memory and learning, the studies also provide insights into why it is so hard for addicts to quit. The association between the sights and smells of a particular place, and the memory of a euphoria-producing behavior is overpowering.

Researchers are trying to identify how environmental cues

produce a biological reaction in addicts who have quit taking drugs years earlier.

One thing they do know is that relapse is also influenced by stress. A brain chemical called corticotropin releasing factor (CRF) that regulates stress plays an important role in limiting reward.

THE "PLEASURE PATHWAY" IN THE BRAIN

Scientists are gaining new insights into the mesolimbic reward system, the brain's "pleasure pathway" that is activated by the release of a common brain chemical, dopamine. Dopamine travels from the ventral tegmental area to the nucleus accumbens and the prefrontal cortex. It is released during normal pleasurable activities, such as eating, socializing or sex.

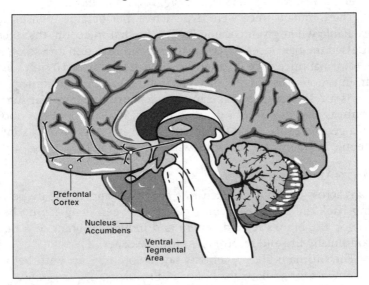

Prefrontal
Cortex

Nucleus
Accumbens

Ventral
Tegmental
Area

Effect of drugs

Addictive drugs—cocaine, heroin, amphetamines, nicotine and alcohol—hijack the reward system and flood the brain with massive amounts of dopamine. As a result, drug users crave the substance to the exclusion of normal activities.

Al Leshner, *New Understanding of Drug Addiction.*

Several other neurochemicals are also involved in the reward system along with dopamine. Opioid peptides are activated by heroin and GABA is stimulated by alcohol.

This month, researchers at Duke University and Columbia

University announced separately that serotonin, another brain chemical, is connected to drug craving in laboratory mice who are given cocaine.

In a study by Duke biologist Marc Caron, researchers bred a special kind of mouse that lacks a transporter to soak up excess levels of dopamine in the brain. Cocaine blocks this transporter and keeps the high of pleasure loose in the brain.

The mutant mice were administered cocaine, but since they lacked the transporter, they should not have wanted the drugs. Instead, the mice kept giving themselves more and more cocaine, pressing the lever frenetically.

The second study at Columbia, researchers created genetically altered mice that were extremely susceptible to cocaine addiction. These mice were born without a receptor for serotonin, which is believed to help control aggression in humans.

These mutant mice were hyperactive, but became even more excitable when given cocaine. To get the first injection, the mice pressed the bar once. Twice for the second injection and so on.

Normal mice gave up after pressing the bar 8 to 10 times for an injection. The altered mice pressed the bar 25 to 30 times.

As a result of these experiments, scientists believe that serotonin is also involved in drug addiction. It also opens the door to a genetic explanation to addiction and may explain why some people instantly crave cocaine, while others don't.

ANTI ADDICTION DRUGS

Labs across the country, like those at Scripps and UCSF, are peeling back the multilayer connections between drug-taking behavior, the brain's reward system and individual brain cells that continually fire and receive chemical messages.

The ultimate goal, scientists say, is to come up with better treatments for addicts, alcoholics and smokers.

Advances in molecular biology in the past decade already have given scientists the location of receptor sites on brain cells that may be good places for potential anti-addiction medications. By blocking these sites, which operate like a molecular lock-and-key mechanism, you could block the effects of addictive substances.

One such anti-cocaine drug is currently undergoing clinic trials.

The real challenge, though, is getting addicts to take medication during the withdrawal period, a time when they are most vulnerable to craving and relapse.

Another research target is the regulation of pleasure. Maybe there is something in the brain that tells us when we're having too much fun. On the other hand, researchers suggest, if there is, there's probably a good evolutionary reason for it.

"If you're a hyena in the jungle and you come across some road kill and eat until you can't move, you're going to be eaten next," Koob said.

Researchers caution that there is no "silver bullet" to vanquishing drug abuse. One obstacle, according to Malenka, is that big drug companies aren't as willing to invest research dollars in helping drug addicts as they are for finding cures for cancer, AIDS or obesity. Funding for Malenka's UCSF center came from the wealthy owner of a Los Angeles water company who had a family member addicted to illicit drugs.

Traditional treatment involves a combination of counseling, getting the addict away from his surroundings, and medications such as methadone for heroin addicts. Methadone actually produces the same dopamine level as heroin, but allows the user to function normally and manage his addiction. Federal law enforcement officials continue to fight the war on drugs with tenacity, but experts believe that the solution is finding out the motivation for addicts' self-destructive behavior.

"The major reason that people take drugs is that they like what it does to their brains," said Alan Leshner, director of the National Institute of Drug Abuse, at the UCSF conference. "Addiction is a brain disease with social aspects. If you want to understand addiction you have to understand that it's a mind-body phenomena."

"The . . . assertion that 'addiction is primarily a brain disease'. . . omits the voluntary aspects of an addict's behavior."

ADDICTION IS NOT A DISEASE

Sally L. Satel

Sally L. Satel argues in the following viewpoint that the biological component of addiction is exaggerated. She maintains that addiction is not a brain disease over which addicts have no control. Although the impact of addictive drugs on the brain makes it difficult for addicts to quit, treatment can help addicts fight cravings and take responsibility for their own behavior. Satel is a psychiatrist who works in a clinic that administers methadone to heroin addicts.

As you read, consider the following questions:

1. What evidence does the author provide to support her claim that addicts have control over their behavior?
2. What comparison does Satel draw between addicts and diabetics or asthmatics?
3. According to the author, what is the best way to combat the stigma of addiction?

Reprinted from Sally Satel, "Don't Forget the Addict's Role," The New York Times, Op-Ed, April 4, 1998, by permission. Copyright ©1998 by The New York Times.

From the first installment of Bill Moyers's widely publicized television special, "Addiction: Close to Home," viewers learned that addiction is a chronic and relapsing brain disease.

The addict's brain "is hijacked by drugs," Mr. Moyers said that morning on "Meet the Press," adding that "relapse is normal."

These are the words of a loving father who was once at his wits' end over his son's drug and alcohol habit. But as a public health message, they miss the mark. First, addiction is not a brain disease. And second, relapse is not inevitable.

THE BIOLOGICAL COMPONENT OF ADDICTION

The National Institute on Drug Abuse, part of the National Institutes of Health, is waging an all-out campaign to label addiction a chronic and relapsing brain disease. It seems a logical scientific leap.

Obviously, heavy drug use affects the brain, often to a point where self-control is utterly lost—for example, when a person is in the throes of alcohol or heroin withdrawal or in the midst of a cocaine binge. Scientists have even identified parts of the brain that "light up," presumably reflecting damage, after long-term exposure to drugs. Yet as dramatic as the images of this phenomenon are, there is wide disagreement on what they mean.

"Saying these changes predict that someone will relapse amounts to modern phrenology," John P. Seibyl, a nuclear radiologist and psychiatrist at the Yale School of Medicine, told me. "We don't have any data linking these images to behavior, so how can we call addiction a disease of the brain?"

ADDICTION AND FREE WILL

One of my colleagues puts it this way: You can examine brains all day, but you'd never call anyone an addict unless he acted like one. That's what is really misleading about the Moyers assertion that "addiction is primarily a brain disease"—it omits the voluntary aspects of an addict's behavior.

Addicts' brains are not always in a state of siege. Many addicts have episodes of clean time that last for weeks, months or years. During these periods it is the individual's responsibility to make himself less vulnerable to drug craving and relapse.

Treatment can help the addict learn how to fight urges and find alternative ways to meet emotional and spiritual needs. But will he take the advice? Maybe. More likely, he will begin a revolving-door dance with the treatment system. A recent study showed that only 1 in every 21 patients complete a year in a treatment clinic. To drop out generally means to relapse.

THE CONSEQUENCES OF REGARDING ADDICTION AS A DISEASE

Regarding addiction as a medical condition reduces the onus of reprehensible behavior. The deviant individual no longer feels personally degraded, and he has no need to sever his ties with the respectable community. Both his less damaged self-esteem and his unbroken connection to the community may help him return to conformity. On the other hand, when persons tempted to violate a social prohibition can justify giving way to that temptation by suggesting that they have a medical problem that they cannot help—"I am an alcoholic"—it surely lowers their threshold of resistance to impulses. Thus the epidemic of addictions feeds on itself, producing more criminal and non-criminal deviance than would otherwise occur. According to the temptation perspective, alcohol abusers, for example, despite withdrawal symptoms, still retain the human capacity to set goals for themselves. Sexual "addicts" do also. When St. Augustine prayed to God to make him chaste and added, "but not yet," he did not think of justifying his promiscuity by claiming that his sexual urges were uncontrollable. The addiction assumption not only excuses behavior that could have been controlled. It may underestimate the altruism of those who do good works; Mother Theresa can be dismissed as having been merely addicted to benevolence.

Ultimately, what fuels the addiction epidemic is the belief that humans are powerless in the face of temptation. But human beings are not dominated by instinct, as lower animals are. We retain the ability, at our best, to override social, psychological, and even biological pressures. In the words of a nineteenth-century poet, himself disabled by tuberculosis of the bone, "I am the master of my fate, I am the captain of my soul."

Jackson Toby, Public Interest, Winter 1998.

"Addicts make decisions about use all the time," Dr. Robert L. DuPont, a former director of the national institute, points out. Researchers have found that the amount of alcohol consumed by alcoholics is related to its cost and the effort required to obtain it. Two decades ago Lee Robins, a professor of psychiatry at Washington University in St. Louis, in a classic study of returning Vietnam veterans, found that only 14 percent of men who were addicted to heroin in Vietnam resumed regular use back home. The culture surrounding heroin use, the price and fear of arrest helped keep the rest off the needle.

Thus drug addicts and alcoholics respond to rewards and consequences, not just to physiology. Relapse should not be regarded as an inevitable, involuntary product of a diseased brain.

Turning addiction into a medical problem serves a purpose, of course. The idea is to reduce stigma and get better financing and more insurance coverage for treatment.

As a psychiatrist, I'm all for treatment, but when the national institute says that addiction is just like diabetes or asthma, it has the equation backward. A diabetic or asthmatic who relapses because he ignores his doctor's advice is more like an addict, as his relapses result from forsaking the behavioral regimens that he knows can keep him clean.

True, former addicts are vulnerable to resuming use—hence the "one day at a time" slogan of Alcoholics Anonymous. But they are by no means destined to do so. The message that addiction is chronic and relapse inevitable is demoralizing to patients and gives the treatment system an excuse if it doesn't serve them well.

A BEHAVIORAL CONDITION

Calling addiction a behavioral condition, as I prefer, emphasizes that the person, not his autonomous brain, is the instigator of his relapse and the agent of his recovery. The experts on Bill Moyers's program say that making addiction more like heart disease or cancer will reduce stigma. They're wrong. The best way to combat stigma is to expect drug users to take advantage of treatment, harness their will to prevent relapse and become visible symbols of hard work and responsibility.

This prescription does not deny the existence of vulnerabilities, biological or otherwise. Instead it makes the struggle to relinquish drugs all the more ennobling.

| "Pot users are 266 times more likely to use cocaine than nonusers."

MARIJUANA IS A GATEWAY TO HIGHLY ADDICTIVE DRUGS

Kevin J. Volpe

In the following viewpoint, Kevin J. Volpe asserts that people who smoke marijuana are far more likely to try highly addictive drugs such as cocaine. According to Volpe, marijuana is the mechanism by which people are introduced to hard drugs. At the time this viewpoint was written, Volpe was a research assistant at the National Defense Council Foundation in Alexandria, Virginia, and a student at Duke University.

As you read, consider the following questions:

1. What percentage of people who use marijuana by age 18 move on to use cocaine, as cited by Volpe?
2. According to the author, what are the detrimental health effects of marijuana use?
3. In Volpe's opinion, what measures should the United States government take to combat drugs?

Reprinted from Kevin Volpe, "Marijuana Use Still a Threat," special report, *The Orlando Sentinel*, May 19, 1996, by permission of the author.

The war on drugs has unwittingly been shifted away from marijuana because of the misconception that it is not particularly harmful.

Marijuana's role as a gateway drug will soon lead to a major cocaine epidemic while the Clinton administration belatedly gets serious about drug use.

Teen-age marijuana use doubled between 1992 and 1994, according to the National Household Survey on Drug Use. Thirty-five percent of high-school seniors have smoked pot, and although this is 15 percent below levels in 1979, the rate of increase shows no sign of tapering off.

MARIJUANA AS A GATEWAY

The Center on Addiction and Substance Abuse reported in 1994 that 43 percent of those who use marijuana by age 18 move on to use cocaine. Pot users are 266 times more likely to use cocaine than nonusers. Marijuana also serves as the mechanism to introduce sellers of hard drugs into the market, studies show.

An aspiring drug dealer begins with marijuana, obtains it for friends, establishes a network, and learns the skills to avoid law enforcement. Once experienced, he begins to sell heavier substances.

FAR FROM HARMLESS

Marijuana activity is far from harmless, as some parents and liberal academics believe.

Legalization proponents who use societal acceptance of alcohol as justification fail to make the distinction between the immediate mind-numbing effects of a drink and the mind-altering effect of a joint. Added to this is increasing evidence that links marijuana use to lung cancer. Health experts estimate that inhaling marijuana has 40 times the detrimental effect of tobacco.

Recent studies show that a marijuana smoker's ability to focus attention is decreased. "Subtle drug-influenced deficits . . . cause important difficulties in adapting to intellectual and interpersonal tasks," stated Dr. Harrison Pope and Deborah Yurgelun-Todd of Massachusetts' McLean Hospital in the *Journal of the American Medical Association*. The manifestation of these results is a sharp increase in "drug driving" and industrial accidents while under the influence.

DRUG USE AND CRIME

The connection between drug use and an increased crime rate is well established. More than 50 percent of high-school students involved in gang activity or caught bringing guns to school also admit to regular marijuana abuse. Smoking a joint is not the harmless pastime that adults remember from the '70s.

The dangers of drugs have been significantly downplayed in popular culture, and the education system should combat this.

"PRIMING" THE BRAIN FOR ADDICTION

A study conducted by an American-Spanish team reported that withdrawing from long-term marijuana use produces the same biochemical changes associated with withdrawal from harder drugs. Those changes can "prime" the pot smoker's brain in a way that makes it more susceptible to other drug abuse.

Steve Wilson, *Arizona Republic*, July 1, 1998.

Although the dangers of marijuana alone justify action, its role as a transitional drug to cocaine is cause for alarm. The United States must increase support for those elements fighting drug production and trafficking. Since 1993, the Clinton administration has cut assistance for combatting drugs to Colombia, Bolivia, and Peru by 36 percent, and stopped sending much-needed US military advisers.

The United States needs to continue to develop and invest in technological surveillance equipment, such as infrared radar and improved X-ray devices for cargo inspections. Former presidential candidate Lamar Alexander's idea for a separate military branch to run counterdrug efforts was reactionary and not well thought out. A better idea would be to combine military and civilian resources under an official joint task force.

Spending cuts made during the past four years in the drug war must be reversed, and renewed attention given to drug awareness programs in our schools.

A casual posture toward teen-age marijuana use now will translate into desperate counterdrug measures later, as addiction further corrodes the economic and social foundation of American culture and threatens the security of our nation.

"Most marijuana users—83 percent—never use cocaine."

MARIJUANA IS NOT A GATEWAY TO HIGHLY ADDICTIVE DRUGS

John Morgan and Lynn Zimmer

John Morgan and Lynn Zimmer maintain in the following viewpoint that no causal link has been established between the use of marijuana and the use of harder drugs. In fact, the vast majority of marijuana users never go on to use hard drugs. Morgan is a professor of pharmacology at the City University of New York Medical School. Zimmer is a sociologist at Queens College in New York. Both serve as directors for the National Organization for the Reform of Marijuana Laws, an organization that works for the legalization of marijuana, and coauthored the 1997 book *Marijuana Myths, Marijuana Facts: A Review of the Scientific Evidence.*

As you read, consider the following questions:

1. According to the authors, why is the statistic that marijuana users are 85 times more likely than non-marijuana users to try cocaine inaccurate?
2. What proof do the authors provide that rates of marijuana use and rates of cocaine use are unrelated?
3. In the authors' view, how does Holland's drug policy eliminate any potential gateway effect of marijuana?

Reprinted from John Morgan and Lynn Zimmer, "Marijuana's Gateway Myth," *Drug Reform Coordination Network Activist Guide*, June 1995, with permission.

The Partnership for a Drug-Free America, in cooperation with the National Institute on Drug Abuse (NIDA) and the White House Office of Drug Control Policy, announced in 1995 an anti-drug campaign that specifically targets marijuana. Instead of featuring horror tales of marijuana-induced insanity, violence and birth defects, this campaign is built upon the premise that reducing marijuana use is a practical strategy for reducing the use of more dangerous drugs.

The primary basis for this "gateway hypothesis" is a report by the Center on Addiction and Substance Abuse (CASA), claiming that marijuana users are 85 times more likely than non-marijuana users to try cocaine. This figure, using data from NIDA's 1991 National Household Survey on Drug Abuse, is close to being meaningless. It was calculated by dividing the proportion of marijuana users who have ever used cocaine (17%) by the proportion of cocaine users who have never used marijuana (.2%). The high risk-factor obtained is a product not of the fact that so many marijuana users use cocaine but that so many cocaine users used marijuana previously.

NOT A "GATEWAY" DRUG

It is hardly a revelation that people who use one of the least popular drugs are likely to use the more popular ones—not only marijuana, but also alcohol and tobacco cigarettes. The obvious statistic not publicized by CASA is that most marijuana users—83 percent—never use cocaine. Indeed, for the nearly 70 million Americans who have tried marijuana, it is clearly a "terminus" rather than a "gateway" drug.

During the last few years, after a decade of decline, there has been a slight increase in marijuana use, particularly among youth. In 1994, 38 percent of high school seniors reported having ever tried the drug, compared to about 35 percent in 1993 and 33 percent in 1992. This increase does not constitute a crisis. No one knows whether marijuana use-rates will continue to rise. But even if they do, it will not necessarily lead to increased use of cocaine.

Since the 1970s, when NIDA first began gathering data, rates of marijuana and cocaine use have displayed divergent patterns. Marijuana prevalence increased throughout the 1970s, peaking in 1979, when about 60 percent of high school seniors reported having used it at least once. During the 1980s, cocaine use increased while marijuana use was declining. Since 1991, when data for the CASA analysis were gathered, marijuana use-rates have increased while cocaine use-rates have remained fairly steady.

A Flawed Approach to Drug Abuse

The ever-changing nature of the statistical relationship between use-rate for marijuana and cocaine indicates the absence of a causal link between the use of these two drugs. Therefore, even if the Partnership campaign were to be effective in reducing marijuana use it would not guarantee a proportional reduction in the number of people who use cocaine. To the extent anti-drug campaigns are effective, they seem to be most effective in deterring those people who would have been fairly low-level users. There is no reason to believe that anti-marijuana messages of any sort would deter many of those marijuana users—currently 17 percent of the total—who also develop an interest in cocaine.

Marijuana as a Scapegoat

Antidrug propaganda hypes marijuana's "mind expanding" powers to imply that once otherwise innocent teens have tasted smoke-induced nirvana, their morals will fall away and they will become uninhibited, irresponsible zombies, suddenly vulnerable to all drugs. This is reefer madness propaganda.

Blaming pot for heroin addiction is a form of denial that prevents us from addressing the real problem. People abuse hard drugs because they hurt inside, due to feeling depressed and isolated. Rather than acknowledge the alienation, the reefer madness argument asks us to blame a plant.

Nori J. Muster, *Pray for Peace Foundation News Opinion*, http://www.snowcrest.net/~swtlight/pfpf.html.

Nor is there reason to believe that the Partnership's campaign will actually reduce the overall number of marijuana users. For over a decade, American youth have been subjected to an unparalleled assault of anti-drug messages. They have seen hundreds of Partnership advertisements, on television and in the print media. They have been urged to "just say no" by rock stars, sports heroes, presidents and first-ladies. They have been exposed to anti-drug educational programs in the schools. Yet this is the same generation of young people that recently began increasing its use of marijuana. It seems unlikely that many of them will be deterred by hyperbolic claims of marijuana's gateway effect, particularly when it contradicts the reality of drug use they see around them.

Separating Drug Markets

If the creators of American drug policy are truly interested in reducing the risk of marijuana users using other drugs, they should take a closer look at Holland, where drug policy since the 1970s has been guided by a commitment to diminishing any potential gateway effect. Wanting to keep young marijuana users away from cocaine and other "hard drugs," the Dutch decided to separate the retail markets by allowing anyone 18 years of age or older to purchase marijuana openly in government-controlled "coffee shops" which strictly prohibit the use and sale of other drugs.

Despite easy availability, marijuana prevalence among 12 to 18 year olds in Holland is only 13.6 percent—well below the 38 percent use-rate for American high school seniors. More Dutch teenagers use marijuana now than in the past; indeed, lifetime prevalence increased nearly three-fold between 1984 and 1992, from 1.0 to 13.6 percent. However, Dutch officials consider their policy a success because the increase in marijuana use has not been accompanied by an increase in the use of other drugs. For the last decade, the rate of cocaine use among Dutch youth has remained stable, with about .3 percent of 12–18 year olds reporting having used it in the past month.

In the United States, the claim that marijuana acts as a gateway to the use of other drugs serves mainly as a rhetorical tool for frightening Americans into believing that winning the war against heroin and cocaine requires waging a battle against the casual use of marijuana. Not only is the claim intellectually indefensible, but the battle is wasteful of resources and fated to failure.

"The earlier a young person drinks alcohol, the more likely he or she is to develop a clinically defined alcohol disorder at some point in life."

UNDERAGE DRINKING INCREASES THE RISK OF ALCOHOLISM

Hazelden Foundation

The Hazelden Foundation asserts in the following viewpoint that underage drinkers have an increased risk of becoming alcoholics later in life. According to research studies, more than 40 percent of people who began drinking before age 15 developed a dependence on alcohol at some point in their lives. The Hazelden Foundation is a nonprofit organization providing rehabilitation, education, prevention, and professional services in the field of chemical dependency.

As you read, consider the following questions:

1. What statistics does the Hazelden Foundation cite to support its claim that underage drinkers are at an increased risk of abusing alcohol later in life?
2. According to the Hazelden Foundation, how much influence do parents have over whether their children decide to drink?

Reprinted, with permission, from "Underage Drinking Is Strong Predictor of Alcoholism, Alcohol Abuse," Alive & Free column, *Hazelden Foundation Newsletter* (1998) at www.hazelden.org/newsletter_detail.dbm?id=459.

The National Institute on Alcohol Abuse and Alcoholism (NIAAA) now has hard evidence to support what many prevention specialists and parents have long assumed: Youthful experimentation with alcohol is not a benign rite of passage. It is a risk-filled practice that can have disastrous results. The earlier a young person drinks alcohol, the more likely he or she is to develop a clinically defined alcohol disorder at some point in life.

A $12-million study by NIAAA offers scientific validation that young people who began drinking before age 15 are four times more likely to develop alcoholism than those who began drinking at age 21. More than 40 percent of respondents who began drinking before age 15 were classified with alcohol dependence at some time in their lives compared with 24.5 percent for respondents who began drinking at age 17 and about 10 percent for those who began drinking at age 21 and 22. The study also found that the risk of developing alcohol abuse (a maladaptive drinking pattern that repeatedly causes life problems) more than doubled for persons who began drinking before age 15 compared with those who began drinking at age 21. The study, which sampled 43,000 people, documents that the risk for alcohol dependence and alcohol abuse decreases steadily and significantly with each increasing year of age of drinking onset. The NIAAA study has become an important teaching tool for people such as Kay Provine, a prevention specialist at Hazelden and codeveloper of a popular parenting skills program called Roots and Wings. "As soon as the study came out, I made a bar graph to show the correlation between early drinking and alcoholism," said Provine. "It is so effective for parents to see something this concrete. Every year you can delay kids from using alcohol you are buying them time to develop physically, emotionally, spiritually and psychologically."

THE EFFECTIVENESS OF PARENTAL OBJECTION

Parents often don't think their kids listen to them, said Provine. But the annual Minnesota Student Survey of 9th and 12th graders conducted for the Minnesota Department of Children, Families and Learning, consistently shows that young people are listening. "Parental objection is the second most important reason kids give for not using alcohol," said Provine. (The first is "don't like the taste.") "Young people are beginning to drink earlier and earlier now—some as young as 9 or 10. And drinking for them is about intoxication, about getting drunk. Each of these facts spells trouble. Parents can consider it a victory of sorts if they can see that their kids delay onset of use, whether it is a matter of months or years. Every day our youth choose not to use improves their chances of not developing alcohol use problems."

Provine and other prevention specialists know that the most effective prevention programs are ongoing, consistent and involve all aspects of a child's life: home, school and community. One program that has been proven to be effective is Project Northland, a community-based prevention program designed to delay the onset of alcohol use, reduce alcohol use for young people who have already tried drinking, and limit the number of alcohol-related problems of young people. Project Northland began at the University of Minnesota in 1990 as a prevention research program funded by the NIAAA. It is the largest randomized community trial ever conducted for the prevention of adolescent alcohol use.

CONSEQUENCES OF ADOLESCENT ALCOHOL USE

Drinking and Driving. Of the nearly 8,000 drivers ages 15–20 involved in fatal crashes in 1995, 20 percent had blood alcohol concentrations above zero.

Sexual Behavior. Surveys of adolescents suggest that alcohol use is associated with risky sexual behavior and increased vulnerability to coercive sexual activity. Among adolescents surveyed in New Zealand, alcohol misuse was significantly associated with unprotected intercourse and sexual activity before age 16. Forty-four percent of sexually active Massachusetts teenagers said they were more likely to have sexual intercourse if they had been drinking, and 17 percent said they were less likely to use condoms after drinking.

Risky Behavior and Victimization. Survey results from a nationally representative sample of 8th and 10th graders indicated that alcohol use was significantly associated with both risky behavior and victimization and that this relationship was strongest among the 8th-grade males, compared with other students.

Puberty and Bone Growth. High doses of alcohol have been found to delay puberty in female and male rats, and large quantities of alcohol consumed by young rats can slow bone growth and result in weaker bones.

National Institute on Alcohol Abuse and Alcoholism, *Alcohol Alert*, July 1997.

Project Northland, designed to be implemented over a three-year period during grades 6–8, involves students, parents, teachers and the community at large. The prevention curriculum, published by Hazelden, uses comic book characters to help young people talk with their parents about alcohol (sixth grade), deal with peer pressures to use alcohol (seventh grade), and develop community-wide changes in alcohol-related programs and policies (eighth grade).

Among 2,400 students followed in northeastern Minnesota, monthly drinking was 20 percent lower and weekly drinking was 30 percent lower for students who engaged in Project Northland activities compared with students in control groups who did not. "Parents have to let their kids know that underage drinking is not okay," said Provine. "They need to talk about family standards and expectations and talk about them again and again. Hopefully, they'll wait to experiment with alcohol. It might not stop the train, but it will put the brakes on."

> "To many Americans, the idea of offering children alcohol is reprehensible. Yet this approach to drinking seems to inoculate children against alcohol abuse later in life."

UNDERAGE DRINKING CAN LOWER THE RISK OF ALCOHOLISM

Stanton Peele

In the following viewpoint, Stanton Peele argues that allowing children to drink can prevent them from abusing alcohol later in life. According to Peele, if children are taught how to drink responsibly, their risk of developing problems with alcohol decreases. To support his claim, he asserts that Mediterranean societies—in which young children are served wine at meals—have much lower rates of alcoholism than societies that urge children to abstain from alcohol. Peele is the author of a number of books on addiction, including *Diseasing of America* and *The Truth About Addiction and Recovery*.

As you read, consider the following questions:

1. As cited by Peele, what does psychiatrist George Vaillant's study conclude about culture attitudes toward alcohol and the risk of alcoholism?
2. According to the author, what is the problem with a blanket disapproval of underage drinking?
3. In Peele's opinion, how do children react to the message that they must abstain from alcohol?

Reprinted from Stanton Peele, "Tell Children the Truth About Drinking," *Los Angeles Times*, March 1, 1996, by permission of the author.

After years of debate, the U.S. government has finally decided that alcohol can be beneficial. Federal dietary recommendations, revised every five years, now indicate that moderate drinking lowers the risk of heart disease. The dietary guidelines note that such "beverages have been used to enhance the enjoyment of meals throughout human history."

There is both old and new information in this statement. We all know that many Americans drink only occasionally or lightly at meals and social occasions. They know when to quit, don't misbehave when they drink and enjoy the taste and sensations of alcohol without going overboard.

Most of us are also aware that people in different cultures handle alcohol differently. In Mediterranean societies—Italy, Spain, Portugal—alcohol is consumed in the form of wine, usually at meals, by family members of all ages. Even small children are served wine on special occasions. Many European countries permit adolescents to drink with their families at restaurants.

INOCULATING CHILDREN AGAINST ALCOHOLISM

To many Americans, the idea of offering children alcohol is reprehensible. Yet this approach to drinking seems to inoculate children against alcohol abuse later in life. A study conducted by Harvard psychiatrist George Vaillant followed a group of men in Boston for more than four decades. The Italian, Greek and Jewish men were only one-seventh as likely as Irish Americans in the study to become alcoholic.

In contemporary America, we are taught that alcoholics are born, not made. Yet no gene determines that any individual will become an alcoholic. Rather, development of adult alcoholism is a long-term, interactive process. Despite our claim to advanced medical knowledge about alcoholism, America produces many more problem drinkers than do many traditional cultures.

TEACHING RESPONSIBLE DRINKING

The groups in the Vaillant study that had few alcoholics actually teach children responsible drinking at home. The problem with a blanket disapproval of drinking is that many children develop drinking habits on their own that are very different from sipping wine at a religious feast or family meal. National surveys show that up to half of college students and high school seniors have drunk five or more drinks at one sitting in the prior two weeks. Among fraternity and sorority members, this figure is 80%.

Ironically, in the United States today, we follow the method of alcohol education found least successful in the Vaillant study.

That is, alcohol is grouped with illicit drugs, and children are taught that abstinence is the only answer. Yet children are aware that most adults drink, and many drink alcohol themselves on the sly. Moreover, drinking will be legal and widely available to them within a few short years. Clearly, many young people find the abstinence message confusing and hypocritical.

THE HEALTH BENEFITS OF ALCOHOL

Studies that examine health outcomes among groups of adults who have been tracked for years find that moderate drinkers live longer than abstainers. What is moderate drinking? The government defined this as no more than two drinks daily for men and one for women. Britain has defined higher sensible drinking limits—two to three drinks for women and three to four for men.

These standards apply to adult men and post-menopausal women, or to any adult with one or more coronary risk factors (such as having a parent with premature heart disease, being overweight, having high cholesterol or blood pressure). Three-quarters of all Americans have such risk factors. These adults show significant reduction in mortality when they drink moderately.

WHY ABSTINENCE IS NOT A REALISTIC GOAL

Drugs have always been and are likely to remain a part of American culture. We routinely alter our states of consciousness through accepted means such as alcohol, tobacco, caffeine, and prescription medications. Americans are perpetually bombarded with messages that encourage them to medicate with a variety of substances. In this context, . . . adolescent experimentation with mind-altering substances is "normal." Since total abstinence is not a realistic goal, we must take a pragmatic rather than moralistic view toward drug use. Like sexual activity, drug use will happen, so instead of becoming morally indignant and punitive, we should assume the existence of drug use and seek to minimize its negative effects.

Marsha Rosenbaum, *National Council on Crime and Delinquency*, August 1996.

The lower death rate among moderate drinkers is due to the reduction in heart disease, specifically atherosclerosis or clogging of the arteries. Alcohol enhances high density—or good— cholesterol production. However, when people average more than two drinks daily, they are more likely to suffer from such diseases as cancer and cirrhosis. At five to six drinks daily for men and four drinks for women, these risks distinctly outweigh the benefits of drinking.

SOUND JUDGMENT AND MODERATION

What are people to make of these complications in the message about alcohol? Like most things in life, sound judgment and moderation are the bywords. After all, there are many things people consume occasionally—such as meat, desserts or cigars—that if done to excess become health problems.

Even adolescents can define the difference between healthy and unhealthy drinking. I recommend holding such open discussions among teenagers in place of the standard temperance lecture that passes for alcohol education. After all, even the government confirms that all drinking is not bad.

Periodical Bibliography

The following articles have been selected to supplement the diverse views presented in this chapter. Addresses are provided for periodicals not indexed in the *Readers' Guide to Periodical Literature*, the *Alternative Press Index*, the *Social Sciences Index*, or the *Index to Legal Periodicals and Books*.

Hillary R. Clinton	"Tools of the Tobacco Industry," *Liberal Opinion*, August 11, 1997. Available from PO Box 468, Vinton, IA 52349.
Don Feder	"Teens and Tobacco: Smoke Gets in Their Eyes," *Conservative Chronicle*, November 8, 1995. Available from PO Box 11297, Des Moines, IA 50340.
Bob Hebert	"In the Mouth of Babes," *Liberal Opinion*, October 28, 1996.
Mark Gauvreau Judge	"Alcoholism: Character or Genetics?" *Insight*, March 3, 1997. Available from 3600 New York Ave. NE, Washington, DC 20002.
John Leo	"Thank You for Not Smoking," *U.S. News & World Report*, July 15–22, 1996.
J. Madeleine Nash	"Addicted," *Time*, May 5, 1997.
Ronald A. Reno	"Gambling Addicts Need Antidote," *Insight*, November 13, 1995.
Joann Ellison Rodgers	"Addiction: A Whole New View," *Psychology Today*, September 1, 1994.
Jill Sell	"Alcoholism: Genetics or the Environment?" *Priorities*, vol. 7, no. 1, 1997. Available from the American Council on Science and Health, 1995 Broadway, 2nd Fl., New York, NY 10023-5860.
Joan Stephenson	"Clues Found to Tobacco Addiction," *JAMA*, April 24, 1996. Available from the American Medical Association, PO Box 10946, Chicago, IL 60610-0946.
Kara Villamil	"Cocaine in the Brain," *World & I*, September 1997. Available from 3600 New York Ave. NE, Washington, DC 20002.

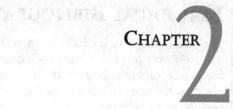

Is Addiction a Serious Problem?

Chapter Preface

According to classic definitions, addiction refers to the compulsive use of a habit-forming substance. The two characterizing features of addiction are tolerance—the need for higher doses of a substance in order to produce the same effects—and the occurrence of withdrawal symptoms upon quitting. Long-term users of heroin, for example, no longer experience a high from heroin but keep taking it in order to ward off painful withdrawal symptoms.

While most people agree that heroin and other "hard" drugs are addictive, any consensus about the definition of addiction ends here. The principal controversy over defining addiction is whether a compulsive interest in activities other than drug use—such as gambling, sex, surfing the Internet, or eating—constitutes addiction.

Some experts maintain that any compulsive behavior—whether it involves the use or drugs or not—signifies an addiction. In fact, these experts maintain, an addiction to the Internet, for example, acts no differently that an addiction to heroin; in both cases, the addiction progresses until it becomes all-consuming. Furthermore, people suffering from non-drug addictions often report symptoms traditionally associated with drug addictions. Sheila Wexler, an expert on compulsive gambling and the wife of an ex-gambler, claims that some gamblers are "so high when they come into treatment, some have to be put into detox. They have elevated blood pressure, dilated pupils, sweats, shakes, extreme states of agitation. This is with no signs of alcohol or drug use in their lab work."

Others argue that the assumption that people are compelled to gamble, eat, surf the Internet—or even smoke—is erroneous. Skeptics of broad definitions of addiction contend that when people engage in habitual behavior, they are exercising free will. Calling them "addicts" falsely implies that they have no control over their own behavior. As columnist George Bain points out, "What is wrong with the current insistence on smoking as addictive, not simply a bad habit, is that the term carries an implication of helplessness."

While some critics view the expansive definition of addiction as a way of absolving people from personal responsibility, others insist that the definition reflects the prevalence of addiction in society. In the following chapter, authors provide opposing views on whether addiction is a serious problem.

| "Illegal drug use among young people
  ages 12 to 17 [is increasing]."

SUBSTANCE ABUSE AMONG TEENS IS RISING

Join Together

In the following viewpoint, Join Together, a national resource center for communities working to reduce substance abuse and gun violence, asserts that the problem of teenage drug abuse is growing. Recent evidence demonstrates that illegal drug use, especially the use of marijuana, is increasingly common among teenagers.

As you read, consider the following questions:

1. As cited by Join Together, what did the National Household Survey on Drug Abuse report about marijuana use among young people?
2. What were the survey's findings about drug use among teens who smoke cigarettes or drink alcohol?

Reprinted from Join Together, "Survey Shows Youth Drug Use Increase," *Join Together Online*, August 21, 1998, www.jointogether.org, with permission.

While illicit drug use among the overall U.S. population remained level from 1996 to 1997, the 1998 National Household Survey on Drug Abuse, conducted by the Substance Abuse and Mental Health Services Administration, found that illegal drug use among young people ages 12 to 17 increased, according to an Aug. 21, 1998, press release from the U.S. Department of Health and Human Services (HHS).

"This study confirms the significant threat from illegal drugs to our children," said Gen. Barry McCaffrey, director of the White House Office on National Drug Control Policy. "We must face this threat head-on, which we intend to do. We embrace today's findings as further proof of the need to fully fund our National Drug Control Strategy. We must expand community coalitions and get the "no drug use" message out to children, their parents and their mentors as President Clinton's strategy requires."

Major Findings of the Survey

Marijuana continues to be the most frequently used illegal drug; the survey found that marijuana use among young people increased from 7.1 percent in 1996 to 9.4 percent in 1997. There was no increase in the use of inhalants, hallucinogens, cocaine or heroin between 1996 and 1997 among 12- to 17-year-olds.

"This survey shows that our work in combating drug use must be focused on our young people," said HHS Secretary Donna E. Shalala. "It shows that abuse of one substance like

" SO THIS IS WHY THEY CALL IT *HIGH SCHOOL!* "

Reprinted by permission of Doug Marlette and Creators Syndicate.

marijuana often goes hand-in-hand with the abuse of other substances. Most of all, this survey says to me that we must work even more closely with parents."

Other findings of the survey with regards to youth in the 12 to 17 age group were: the rate of current alcohol use was about 50 percent in 1979, but fell to about 21 percent in 1992, and has remained relatively stable; drug use was higher among those who were currently using cigarettes and alcohol, compared with youths not using these substances; and in 1997, 11.4 percent of youth reported using illicit drugs in the past month, an increase from 9.0 percent in 1996.

"[A recent survey] found that while marijuana use continued to rise among 10th and 12th graders in 1997, use of other drugs began to level off."

SUBSTANCE ABUSE AMONG TEENS IS NOT RISING

Sharon Cargo

Sharon Cargo reports in the following viewpoint that teenage drug and alcohol abuse has begun to level off. According to Cargo, the slowdown in rates of adolescent substance abuse reflects an increased disapproval of drugs, alcohol, and tobacco among teens. Cargo is a contributing writer for NIDA Notes, a publication of the National Institute on Drug Abuse.

As you read, consider the following questions:

1. According to the 1997 survey cited by Cargo, what are the general trends in drug use among eighth, tenth, and twelfth graders?
2. What recent trends in teen alcohol use does the author report?
3. What evidence does the author provide that teen attitudes about drug use, frequent drinking, and cigarette smoking are changing?

Reprinted from Sharon Cargo, "Increases in Teen Drug Use Appear to Level Off," NIDA Notes, vol. 13, no. 2, October 1998, at www.nida.nih.gov/NIDA_Notes/NNVol13N2/level.html.

R ates of increase in illicit drug use among the Nation's high school students showed some signs of slowing between 1996 and 1997, according to NIDA's [the National Institute on Drug Abuse] annual Monitoring the Future study, which is conducted by the Institute for Social Research at the University of Michigan. The survey, released in December 1997, found that while marijuana use continued to rise among 10th and 12th graders in 1997, use of a number of other drugs began to level off. Drug use among 8th graders actually decreased somewhat. Approximately 51,000 8th-, 10th-, and 12th-grade students in more than 400 public and private schools participated in the 1997 survey.

Current use of any illicit drug—defined as using drugs at least once in the past 30 days—decreased among 8th graders from 14.6 percent in 1996 to 12.9 percent in 1997. Current use of illicit drugs among 10th graders held steady at 23 percent. Twelfth graders showed no significant increase in current drug use. Rates of increases for 12th graders have slowed each year since 1992.

"The possible slowdown of illicit drug use among young people is encouraging even though rates of use remain unacceptably high," says Health and Human Services Secretary Dr. Donna E. Shalala. "All of us, especially parents and teachers, need to redouble our efforts to make young people understand that drug abuse is illegal, dangerous, and wrong."

MARIJUANA

Among 8th graders, overall marijuana use held steady or decreased rather than increased for the first time since 1992. The percentage of 8th-grade students who reported daily marijuana use showed a decrease, from 1.5 percent in 1996 to 1.1 percent in 1997. The percentage who reported having used marijuana annually or at least once in their lives—called "lifetime use" in the survey—did not change significantly. Some 17.7 percent said they used marijuana annually, and 10.2 percent said they currently used the drug.

Annual and current use of marijuana among 12th graders did not change significantly between 1996 and 1997. However, their lifetime marijuana use rose significantly from 44.9 percent to 49.6 percent, and daily use increased to 5.8 percent in 1997, up from 4.9 percent in the year before. Among 10th graders, lifetime marijuana use increased to 42.3 percent from 39.8 percent in 1996.

Rates of daily cigarette smoking followed a trend similar to daily marijuana smoking with decreases among 8th graders, increases among 12th graders, and no significant change among 10th graders.

Alcohol use remained generally stable in all three grades, with 8th graders showing some improvement. In 1997, 8.2 percent of 8th graders reported having been drunk within the 30 days before the survey, a decrease from 9.6 percent the year before. No significant changes took place in the percentages of 10th and 12th graders reporting drunkenness in the 30 days before the survey.

TRENDS IN TEENS' CURRENT USE OF ANY ILLICIT DRUGS

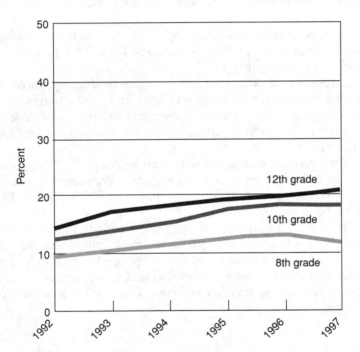

The percentage of 10th and 12th graders who reported having used any illicit drug within the last 30 days—called current use—did not increase significantly from 1996 to 1997. The percentage of 8th graders reporting current use decreased by 1.7%.

Rates of cocaine use remained level for 8th- and 10th-grade students, but among 12th graders lifetime use of cocaine in all forms increased. The percentage of seniors who said that they had used cocaine at least once increased from 7.1 percent in 1996 to 8.7 percent in 1997, the highest rate reported since

1990. In 1997, 2.1 percent of 8th, 10th, and 12th graders reported having used heroin at least once in their lives.

SHIFTING ATTITUDES

The slowdown in drug use among 8th graders reflects a shift in attitudes. For the first time since 1991, the survey detected an increase in 8th graders' disapproval of drug use. There was increased disapproval of regular marijuana and smokeless tobacco use, frequent drinking and cigarette smoking, and any use of heroin. For example, in 1996, 76.5 percent of 8th graders said they disapproved or strongly disapproved of occasional marijuana use, but in 1997, the number climbed to 78.1 percent. However, fewer 8th graders perceived using marijuana once or twice as being potentially harmful. Eighth graders' disapproval of frequent cigarette smoking—defined in the study as smoking one or more packs per day—increased from 77.3 percent in 1996 to 80.3 percent in 1997.

Disapproval of occasional marijuana use and heavy smoking remained about the same among 10th and 12th graders. The one exception: 10th graders were more disapproving of frequent cigarette smoking, up from 71.6 percent in 1996 to 73.8 percent in 1997.

"The apparent shift in attitudes and leveling off of drug use provide additional evidence that drug abuse prevention activities may be taking hold with young people," says NIDA Director Dr. Alan I. Leshner.

"However, the history of drug use trends has shown that once changes in attitudes begin to occur, it is critical that we not just maintain current levels of effort. We need to redouble our prevention efforts to keep any momentum going. And all sectors need to be working together and conveying similar, accurate antidrug messages."

"Tobacco dependency is the most
lethal and the most difficult
addiction to control."

SMOKING CAUSES A DANGEROUS NICOTINE ADDICTION

William Everett Bailey

William Everett Bailey argues in the following viewpoint that
nicotine is more addictive and more dangerous than any other
abused substance. Furthermore, Bailey notes, while other addictive drugs have some beneficial properties, nicotine is destructive in all respects. Bailey, a tobacco control advocate, is the author of The Invisible Drug, from which the following viewpoint is
excerpted.

As you read, consider the following questions:

1. According to Bailey, what are the three hallmarks of nicotine
   addiction?
2. What percentage of smokers want to quit, in Bailey's
   assessment?
3. In the author's view, how does nicotine disturb the brain's
   equilibrium?

Excerpted from William Everett Bailey, The Invisible Drug. Copyright ©1996, Mosaic
Publications, Inc. Reprinted by permission of Mosaic Publications, Inc.

Anyone familiar with botanical insecticides knows that nicotine is a good one. It is sprayed on plants as a freebase concentrate spray. It kills aphids, but it can also kill the person doing the spraying. The lethal dose of nicotine is ten times less that of pyrethrum or rotenone, making it one of the most toxic insecticides.

How much nicotine does it take to kill a human? According to R.H. Dreisbach, author of *Handbook of Poisoning*, one drop of pure nicotine, about 40 mg., placed on the tongue will kill in five minutes. One small drop is the amount of nicotine in about four cigarettes.

Nicotine first stimulates, then depresses and paralyzes the cells of the brain, spinal cord, and nervous system. Next, the skeletal muscles and the diaphragm (breathing muscles) are paralyzed. Death results from respiratory failure.

Two men recently found out how dangerous nicotine is during a smoking contest in China. They smoked two or three at a time continuously until one gave up. One smoked 50 cigarettes and lived to tell about it. Unfortunately, the other man smoked 100 and fell dead from nicotine poisoning.

THE POWER OF NICOTINE ADDICTION

Today, there are millions of drug addicts in America. Most are addicted to nicotine, alcohol, cocaine, and opiate drugs, like morphine. Cocaine and morphine have some medicinal uses and they don't cause cancer. Morphine is safe when given in an appropriate dose and by a safe method to a normal, healthy individual. A life of morphine addiction is socially unacceptable. On the other hand, a life of addiction to a socially acceptable poison that causes cancer is a nightmare.

Drug addiction is not only about the stereotypical street junky. "A drug does not have to be intoxicating to be deemed addictive," says Dr. Jack E. Henningfield, Ph.D., Chief of Clinical Pharmacology Research at the National Institute on Drug Abuse.

The American Psychiatric Association defines addiction as "a compulsive use of a drug resulting in loss of control over intake." The three hallmarks of nicotine addiction that are present in animal experiments are:
- Self-Administration
- Tolerance
- Withdrawal

The scientific criteria for addiction, met by barbiturates, amphetamines, morphine, heroin, alcohol and cocaine, is also met by nicotine. Nicotine addiction is the reason most people smoke. . . .

Some characteristics of nicotine addiction, such as compulsive use, drug-seeking behavior, and physical dependence, can be observed at the entrance of any busy office building. The smokers are huddled outside of their "smoke-free" workplace even in extremely miserable weather to feed their nicotine addiction.

Most heroin addicts will identify their favorite drug as nicotine. Researchers asked heroin addicts, "What drug do you need the most?" from a list including heroin, nicotine, marijuana, amphetamine, barbiturates, LSD, and alcohol. They chose nicotine over all other drugs. Heroin addicts say they needed nicotine the most to cope. Despite successful treatment for their dependency of alcohol and/or drugs, most of these patients will not quit smoking, and most will die from tobacco-related illnesses. Research done at the Mayo Clinic observed the mortality rate of these patients to be 48.1%, much higher than the expected normal mortality rate of 18.5%. From a clinical point of view, tobacco dependency is the most lethal and the most difficult addiction to control.

A DIFFICULT HABIT TO KICK

Smokers also find it difficult to quit. Seventy percent of people who smoke (some 32,000,000 smokers) want to quit. Even after a heart attack or cancer surgery, most want to quit, but can't. Seventy percent of the smokers who survive a heart attack start smoking again within one year. Forty percent of the cancer patients who have undergone surgery continue to smoke.

Visitors to the M.D. Anderson Cancer Center in Houston, a smoke-free hospital, can observe another characteristic of nicotine addiction. In the evenings, patients gather in the parking garage for a smoke. Some are pulling chemotherapy IV pumps behind them. You might see the classic picture of someone smoking through a hole in their throat called a "stoma." They continue to smoke despite having their cancerous larynx removed. This is further testimony to the power of nicotine addiction. . . .

NICOTINE ADDICTION IN CHILDREN

More teens are smoking every day. There were approximately 2.6 million children between the ages of 12 and 17 addicted to nicotine in 1989. In 1993, that number had grown to over three million. Not only are more smoking, but they are starting younger. Smoking increased 30% in the 13 to 14 year group, between 1991 and 1994.

"There is evidence that it is easier to become addicted to nicotine than heroin or cocaine," explains Dr. John Slade, M.D., a Robert Wood Johnson Medical School physician and drug researcher. First time smokers usually go through a sequence of decisions before their first cigarette. For those that decide to try smoking, after smoking four or five consecutive cigarettes, they have a 94% chance of becoming a long-term nicotine addict. Of the 3,000 teens that start smoking every day, nine of every ten will become addicted and half will smoke for 20 years. . . .

NICOTINE TARGETS THE BRAIN

Brown & Williamson Tobacco Co. (B.A.T.) researchers were writing about how nicotine stimulates the brain as early as 1962: "The hypothalamo-pituitary stimulation of nicotine is the beneficial mechanism which makes people smoke." It was not until recently however, that the pharmacological basis of how nicotine works on the brain was discovered. In 1995, the journal Science published research showing evidence of nicotine receptors (nicotinic acetylcholine receptors) in the reward system of the brain called the limbic system.

Neurotransmitters are chemicals that brain cells use to communicate with each other. They act on small "on-off switches" on brain cells called receptors. Nicotine increases the flow of the neurotransmitter glutamate in the limbic system, which indicates that the reward center has been stimulated. Dr. Lorna W. Role, a cell biologist research author at Columbia University in New York, says that a faster flow of glutamate "is like turning up the volume on a radio." Nicotine stimulates the reward system, telling the person "That was good, do it again."

SURVEY OF TEEN SMOKERS	
Tried to quit, but can't.	57% to 75%
Regret they ever started smoking.	70%

"Nicotine commandeers the normal pathways of reward," explains Dr. John Dani, a researcher at Baylor College of Medicine in Houston. It commands you to repeat the action, to keep the nicotine flowing into the bloodstream. "Nicotine tells you to keep on smoking." Nicotine becomes the dangling carrot, and the smoker makes constant effort to get it.

When one continues smoking, the balance of neurotransmitters in the brain begins to change, and the brain becomes accustomed to it. The brain tries to return to normal and modifies enzymes to compensate. For the brain to then work properly, it must have a constant supply of nicotine. This unconscious desire explains the addiction of the individual to nicotine. Tobacco company researchers at B.A.T. in 1962 concluded: "A body left in this unbalanced status craves for renewed drug intake [nicotine] in order to restore the physiological equilibrium."

To restore the balance in the brain, a regular smoker may need nicotine as often as every thirty minutes. Nicotine addiction requires the highest frequency of administration, far exceeding the demands of a cocaine, alcohol, or heroin addiction.

| "If nicotine is addictive, so are chocolate candies, pies, and cakes."

NICOTINE IS NOT THE ACTIVE INGREDIENT IN TOBACCO SMOKE

Lauren A. Colby

In the following viewpoint, Lauren A. Colby questions whether smokers are addicted to nicotine. According to Colby, the assumption that smokers smoke to obtain nicotine is false. If nicotine were really the active ingredient in tobacco products, then nicotine patches would make it possible for all smokers to quit. Colby is the author of In Defense of Smokers, from which the following selection is excerpted.

As you read, consider the following questions:

1. According to Colby, how much nicotine do Havana cigars contain?
2. What evidence does Colby provide to support his claim that nicotine is not the active ingredient in tobacco products?

Excerpted from Lauren A. Colby, In Defense of Smokers, at www. lcolby.com/b-chap11.htm. Reprinted with permission.

M uch of the rhetoric of the anti-smoking movement seeks to demonize tobacco smokers as "nicotine addicts." In the past, of course, the term "addict" has been generally applied only to mind-altering drugs, e.g., heroin and cocaine. Even alcohol, which is mind-altering, is not generally referred to as "addictive." So, the argument is one of semantics. If nicotine is addictive, so are chocolate candies, pies and cakes, etc. Indeed, if "addiction" is defined as dependence upon some chemical, everyone is addicted, to air!

I am not going to engage in a philosophical debate over the definition of "addiction." There is a question in my mind, however, as to whether nicotine is really the active ingredient in tobacco smoke.

WHAT IS NICOTINE?

Nicotine is a chemical, $C_{10}H_{14}N_2$, which is found in the tobacco plant. Anti-smokers are quick to point out that pure nicotine is a poison, used as a pesticide. And it's true that pure nicotine (a colorless, odorless liquid), is poisonous. According to one source, to kill a 180 lb. man, he'd have to drink about 80 mg of the stuff. Many other common substances, however, also have minimum lethal doses. According to the same source, ingesting a gram of caffeine is fatal.

In fact, many substances which are beneficial in small quantities are toxic in large quantities. My mother suffered a stroke some years ago. Her life was saved, and she recovered by taking a blood thinner, so the doctor doubled it. My mother began hemorrhaging and almost died from loss of blood. The blood thinner, which is life-saving in small quantities, proved toxic in large quantities.

Of course, most of the nicotine in tobacco is lost in the process of smoking. Only a little finds its way into the smoker's bloodstream. That small quantity may account for some of the beneficial effects of smoking, e.g., improved mental concentration. Strangely, fine Havana cigars, when they were available, contained only 2% nicotine. If, in fact, nicotine is the reason why people smoke, it seems strange that people would pay enormous amounts of money for Havana cigars, which contain so little nicotine.

NOT AN ACTIVE INGREDIENT

I question, however, whether nicotine is the active ingredient in tobacco. If it were, nicotine patches should satisfy a smoker's craving for tobacco; they don't! In prisons, where, as a part of the punishment, smoking is sometimes forbidden, the inmates take to smoking corn silk, paper, string, etc., none of which contain any nicotine.

When I was a young man, there was a chain of tobacco stores which sold cheap cigars. They were made almost entirely from brown paper, with only one outside wrapper made from tobacco. I doubt they contained any significant amount of nicotine. Yet they were a satisfying smoke.

NOT INESCAPABLE SERVITUDE

Addiction as a physiological phenomenon is real enough, but it is not inescapable servitude. There is no substance so addictive that scores of thousands of people have not been able to stop taking it. . . .

Coerced addiction, if it exists at all, is never at the hands of tobacco companies. The companies have never had goon squads to force us to light up, or to prevent us from giving up once we have started to smoke. In fact, it takes some determination to become addicted to tobacco: one has to overcome an initial natural reluctance to draw smoke into the lungs. And even once addiction has become established, it can be overcome by determination alone, as millions of people have successfully demonstrated.

Anthony Daniels, *National Review*, July 28, 1997.

Recently, anti-smoking forces have suggested taking the nicotine out of cigarettes to discourage smoking. This assumes, of course, that smokers smoke to get nicotine. In their book, *Life Extension*, health writers Durk Pearson and Sandy Shaw take a different approach. Believing that smoke is bad for health but that nicotine is not, Pearson and Shaw suggest that cigarettes be spiked with extra nicotine so that smokers will consume fewer cigarettes.

It is not universally accepted, however, that nicotine is the active ingredient in tobacco smoke. The authors of the widely respected *Merck Manual* say only that it is "probably" the active ingredient. If, in fact, the anti-smokers finally succeed in getting the tobacco companies to remove the nicotine from cigarettes, we will finally find out the truth. My own bet is that a cigarette without nicotine will probably be almost as satisfying as one with nicotine. The active ingredient in smoke is smoke.

"More recent research, however, indicates that the real active ingredient in tobacco smoke may be a monoamine oxidase inhibitor (MAO). MAO inhibitors are anti-depressants; they relax and clam. The prescription smoke-cessation drug Zyban contains such an inhibitor. A naturally occurring MAO inhibitor in tobacco smoke may be the real reason why people smoke, not nicotine."

"The fastest growing addiction in the U.S. is gambling."

COMPULSIVE GAMBLING IS A NATIONAL CONCERN

Bernard P. Horn

In the following viewpoint, Bernard P. Horn, political director for the National Coalition Against Legalized Gambling in Washington, DC, contends that gambling is an addiction of epidemic proportions. Horn maintains that compulsive gambling leads to higher rates of domestic violence, suicide, and crime. The expansion of legalized gambling creates more addicts, many of whom are teenagers.

As you read, consider the following questions:

1. How has legalized gambling expanded since the mid-1970s, according to Horn?
2. In the author's view, how does pathological gambling affect the gambler's entire family?
3. What impact does gambling have on crime, as reported by Horn?

Excerpted from Bernard P. Horn, "Is There a Cure for America's Gambling Addiction?" *USA Today* magazine, May 1997. Reprinted with permission from the Society for the Advancement of Education.

Americans are familiar with the nation's major addictions: narcotics, alcohol, and tobacco. Society has spent countless millions of dollars warning about these substances, and the educational campaigns have had a profound effect.

Today, however, the fastest growing addiction in the U.S. is gambling. There are millions of adult pathological gamblers in America and, more ominous, millions of teenagers are addicted as well.

Individuals are not alone in their addiction. State governments have become hooked on the revenues derived from casinos, slot machines, keno, and lotto. Thus, instead of warning citizens, many governments are exploiting them. They ignore the social costs brought about by state-authorized gambling because they need the cash to balance their budgets—or so they believe.

THE HISTORY OF LEGALIZED GAMBLING

Two decades ago, commercial gambling casinos were prohibited in every state except Nevada. Just 13 states had lotteries. There was no such thing as an Indian casino. Altogether, Americans wagered about $17,000,000,000 on legal commercial gambling.

Between 1976 and 1988, casinos were legalized in Altantic City and the number of state lotteries more than doubled. Since 1988, 19 states legalized casinos and 10 legalized video poker or slot machines at racetracks and bars. All told, Americans will wager more than $550,000,000,000 on legal gambling this year—a 3,200% increase since 1976.

In 1975, the Federal government allowed state lotteries to advertise on television and radio for the first time, resulting in a flood of commercials promoting gambling. What once was considered unacceptable behavior became not only tolerated, but encouraged. As attitudes changed, so did the games. Government offered more opportunities to bet, with faster action and bigger prizes.

In 1987, the Supreme Court, in California v. Cabazon Band of Mission Indians, ruled that Native Americans, without state regulation, could offer legal gambling on Indian reservations if such games were permitted anywhere in the state, in any form. What this meant, in effect, was that if a state allowed volunteer fire departments to conduct occasional low-stakes Las Vegas nights, then an Indian tribe in that state could sponsor 24-hour, high-stakes casino gambling. . . .

LEGALIZED GAMBLING AND ADDICTION

For years, lawmakers forgot why gambling was considered a "vice." In fairness to them, there weren't a lot of objective studies available on the consequences of legalized gambling. The many new gambling outlets sparked opportunities for social and economic research. By 1994, a considerable body of evidence showed that the expansion of legalized gambling destroys individuals, wrecks families, increases crime, and ultimately costs society far more than the government makes.

It is important to understand that gambling addiction is just as real, and its consequences just as tragic, as alcohol or drug abuse. The American Psychiatric Association and the American Medical Association recognize pathological (or "compulsive") gambling as a diagnosable mental disorder.

COMPULSIVE GAMBLING AND CRIMINAL ACTIVITY

In a report for Focus on the Family, Ronald Reno quotes from a survey of pathological gamblers that found that 75 percent of pathological gamblers have committed a felony to support their habit. Henry Lesieur, a criminal justice expert at Illinois State University, says that problem gamblers engage in $1.3 billion of insurance fraud yearly. Which is not surprising, as Lesieur also estimates that the average gambler with a problem has from $53,000 to $92,000 in gambling-related debts.

Blake Hurst, *American Enterprise*, March/April 1996.

Experts on pathological gambling have shown that the prevalence of this disorder is linked closely to the accessibility and acceptability of gambling in society. Like alcoholism, just a small percentage of Americans are susceptible. As more people try gambling in its various forms, however, more of those prone to the illness are exposed. So, the more legalized gambling a state makes available, the more pathological behavior is triggered. Fast-paced gambling, which maximizes the number of wagering opportunities (like casinos and video gambling machines), also maximizes gambling addiction. In 1976, a national commission found that 0.77% of the adults in the U.S., about 1,100,000 Americans, were pathological gamblers. Today, the situation is far worse.

In Iowa, the legalization of casinos more than tripled the addiction dilemma. A study released in July, 1995, found that 5.4% of the state's adults (roughly 110,000 residents) are lifetime pathological or problem gamblers. Before riverboats came to the state, 1.7% of Iowans fell into this category.

In Louisiana, four years after the state legalized casinos and slots, a study found that seven percent of adults had become addicted to gambling. In Minnesota, as 16 Indian casinos opened across the state, the number of Gamblers Anonymous groups shot up from one to 49.

Whether roulette, slots, or lotteries, the odds always favor the house. The more one gambles against these odds, the more certain it becomes that one will lose. When pathological gambling strikes, it rarely affects just one person. Family savings are lost, college education or retirement funds disappear, and home mortgages are foreclosed. Under the stress of losing everything, many problem gamblers commit domestic violence. Since casinos came to the Mississippi Gulf Coast, domestic violence has increased 69% and an estimated 37% of all pathological gamblers have abused their children.

Pathological gamblers lose all the money they have, then run up credit card debt. They sell or pawn possessions and plead for loans from family and friends. More than half end up stealing money, often from their employers. The average Gamblers Anonymous member will have lost all his or her money and accumulated debts ranging from $35,000 to $92,000 before seeking treatment. Thousands file for bankruptcy. Many addicts who can't be helped commit suicide.

CREATING A GENERATION OF ADDICTS

Researchers call gambling the fastest growing teenage addiction, with the rate of pathological gambling among high school and college-aged youth about twice that of adults. According to Howard J. Shaffer, director of the Harvard Medical School Center for Addiction Studies, "Today, there are more children experiencing adverse symptoms from gambling than from drugs . . . and the problem is growing."

Teenage gambling addiction has been inflamed by the expansion of legalized gambling. As Shaffer points out, "There is an emerging body of evidence suggesting that illicit gambling among young people is increasing at a rate at least proportional to the opportunity to gamble legally."

Despite laws in Atlantic City restricting casino gambling to people 21 or older, a survey of teenagers at Altantic City High School revealed that not only had 64% gambled in a local casino, but 40% had done so before the age of 14. Every year, Altantic City casino security personnel report ejecting about 20,000 minors. Just imagine how many thousands more are never caught.

Numerous studies have focused on the link between gambling establishments and crime. Just as Willie Sutton robbed banks because, as he explained, "that's where the money is," so do contemporary crooks target casinos.

Less well-known is the extent to which gambling addiction is turning people into criminals. More than half of all pathological gamblers will commit felonies to pay off gambling debts, particularly financial crimes like embezzlement, check kiting, tax evasion, and credit card, loan, and insurance fraud. Moreover, these tend to be people who never before have committed a crime. Pathological gamblers are responsible for an estimated $1,300,000,000 worth of insurance-related fraud per year.

In 1994, the Florida Office of Planning and Budgeting conducted a study to project the costs of legalizing casino gambling in the state. The biggest potential government expense turned out to be that of incarcerating all the new pathological gamblers who turn to crime. According to the study, "Not counting costs of prosecution, restitution or other related costs, incarceration and supervision costs alone for problem gambler criminal incidents could cost Florida residents $6,080,000,000."

Proponents claim that casinos or slot machines will stimulate jobs and economic growth. The reality is that gambling steals customers from existing businesses, cannibalizing their revenues. As Prof. John Warren Kindt testified before the Small Business Committee of the U.S. House of Representatives, "Traditional businesses in communities which initiate legalized gambling activities can anticipate increased personnel costs due to increased job absenteeism and declining productivity. The best blue-collar and white-collar workers, type-A personalities, are the most likely to become pathological gamblers. A business with 1,000 workers can anticipate increased personnel costs of $500,000 or more per year—simply by having various forms of legalized gambling activities accessible to its workers." No wonder that, soon after casinos were legalized in the resort town of Deadwood, S.D., gambling became one of the top reasons for business bankruptcy in the region.

CASINOS DEPEND ON GAMBLING ADDICTS

Certainly, the managers of gaming establishments, seeing these addicts every day, understand what is going on. In Atlantic City, for instance, after pathological gamblers lose all their cash, empty their ATM accounts from the casino's teller machines, and can borrow no more, they walk outside the casinos to sell their jewelry and other valuables. Selling jewelry is such a big business in Atlantic City that there are about three dozen "Cash for Gold" stores near the entrances to the Boardwalk casinos.

How many tens of thousands of people must sell their valuables each year in order to keep these three dozen establishments in business? (You can get about $15 for a man's gold wedding ring.) Why don't the Atlantic City casinos try to help these miserable customers of theirs?

A simple answer was suggested in testimony before the U.S. House Judiciary Committee: The casinos don't want to stop gambling addiction because they depend on addicts for a huge percentage of their profits. Prof. Earl Grinols presented evidence that pathological and problem gamblers, representing four percent of the adult population, may account for as much as 52% of an average casino's revenues. "In this respect," he noted, "casino gambling resembles alcohol, for which 6.7% of the population consumes 50% of all alcohol consumed.

When an industry literally is exploiting the mentally ill for profit, one might expect government to intervene. However, governments have become addicted to winning the money that addicted gamblers lose.

"Less than 2 percent of gamblers end up hooked."

COMPULSIVE GAMBLING IS NOT A NATIONAL CONCERN

Dick Boland

Dick Boland asserts in the following viewpoint that compulsive gambling is not a serious problem. According to the author, the notion that compulsive gambling is a "disease" and that gamblers cannot control their behavior is absurd. Boland is a nationally syndicated columnist.

As you read, consider the following questions:

1. In the author's opinion, why is gambling a better bet than buying insurance?
2. What percentage of people who enter Gamblers Anonymous regress, as cited by Boland?
3. What rationalization is used by people who overdo, according to the author?

Reprinted from Dick Boland, "Gambling—Addiction of the Nineties," *Conservative Chronicle*, February 18, 1998, by permission of Dick Boland and Creators Syndicate.

In the past, when someone did something to excess, it was called bad judgment. Now, as we all know, if you overdo it, it is called an addiction.

Smoking, eating, drinking, you name it and you will find a group out there trying to save the unfortunate victims of poor judgment from their addiction.

The Crusade Against Gamblers

This week, we have the National Gambling Impact Study Commission looking into the addiction of the '90s. This is the beginning of a crusade to save those individuals who cannot control their desire to beat the house.

They tell us that there was heart-wrenching testimony from 10 recovering compulsive gamblers, pointing out the evils of defying the odds trying to get rich. One compulsive gambling expert calls it a "national health" problem.

This nonsense is the first step toward elimination of casinos by those who are trying to return us to a lifestyle lived by the Puritans in New England, who eventually died out due to boredom. I am sure there are a few people who bet too much and ruin their lives. There are also people who drive too fast and ruin a lot of lives, but there are no anti-driving groups as yet.

The gambling experts said that neither the casino industry, government nor insurance companies are doing enough to help those afflicted with the gambling "disease." What is amazing about that statement is the inclusion of insurance companies. People who never dream of gambling at a casino, nor betting on a sporting event, have no hesitation when it comes to betting on how long they will live or whether or not their house will burn down. Insurance companies put the casino business to shame when it comes to taking a bet.

There are many examples of people who are overinsured to the point where their quality of life is affected drastically. However, I don't believe there is any halfway house available to help wean these individuals off their addiction. While you can't beat the odds at the casino, you get a much better deal than you do at the insurance companies. On occasion a casino will fail, but it is rare to find an insurance company going under.

"It's Not My Fault"

Gamblers Anonymous says that 92 percent of the people who enter their program regress. We are led, once again, to believe that we cannot control our actions and that only our government can help. It's the old "it's not my fault" rationalization used to excess by people who overdo. If we can compare gambling to drug addiction, then why not look at golf or bowling, as well. Many families have suffered hardship because the husband spent most of his money and time trying to lower his handicap.

FALSE SUSPICIONS ABOUT GAMBLING

Government policy on gambling has gone through successive cycles of liberalization, backlash, and renewed prohibition. In the U.S., we are currently experiencing the third nationwide backlash—the first was in the middle of the nineteenth century, the second during the 1940s.

The ease with which public opinion can be mobilized against gambling reflects a deep-rooted suspicion. Most people enjoy gambling in moderation, and will gamble occasionally if they can. Yet these same people often oppose further liberalization of the gambling laws. Gambling is one of those things which are obviously harmless when you or I do them, but fraught with menace if millions of other people can do them too.

Why is gambling, enjoyed by the vast majority of people, denounced day in and day out, with hardly any voices to be heard in its defense? The reigning ideology tells us all that gambling is evil, for several reasons. Gambling is selfish; it is addictive; it provides "false hope"; it is a dangerous competitor to some forms of religion because it too offers the prospect of a greatly improved future life at rather long odds. . . .

Claims about the injurious effects of gambling don't seem to be factually correct. Freedom to gamble encourages hard work on the part of gamblers, especially those with low incomes, just as, broadly speaking, any enhanced opportunity to spend one's earnings as one pleases increases the incentive effect of a given wage. And gambling by itself does not attract crime: it is the illegality of some or all gambling which forces gambling to become a criminal activity.

David Ramsay Steele, Liberty, September 1997.

If gambling truly is a national health problem, what are the odds of Medicare picking up the costs of getting a cure? I would say they are about the same as the insurance companies lowering your premiums on your life insurance as you get older.

The American Gaming Association says that less than 2 percent of gamblers end up hooked. If they want to do something good for gamblers, try making the streets safe for the winners so they can get to their cars.

"Nearly 13.8 million Americans 18 years and older have problems with drinking."

ALCOHOLISM IS A SERIOUS PROBLEM

W. Waldo

In the following viewpoint, W. Waldo contends that alcoholism is a dangerous addiction that progresses over time, ruining the alcoholic's career, family life, and health. Furthermore, alcohol abuse contributes significantly to the incidence of homicide, domestic violence, robbery, and other crimes. W. Waldo is the web publisher of Hope and Healing webChronicles, a resource for information on the spiritual nature of disease.

As you read, consider the following questions:

1. According to W. Waldo, what role does drinking play in an alcoholic's life?
2. How does alcohol abuse affect the health of drinkers, as reported by W. Waldo?
3. In the author's view, what factors contribute to alcoholism?

Reprinted from W. Waldo, "What Is Alcoholism?" *Hope and Healing webChronicles*, www.hopeandhealing.com/eguide20.htm, by permission of the author.

Jointly, the National Council on Alcoholism and Drug Dependence and the American Society of Addiction Medicine defines alcoholism as "a primary, chronic disease with genetic, psychosocial and environmental factors influencing its development and manifestations. Alcoholism is characterized by a continuous or periodic impaired control over drinking; preoccupation with alcohol; and use of alcohol despite adverse consequences and distortions in thinking, most notably denial."

From the first drink, alcohol consumption for the alcoholic is different from that of a non-alcoholic. For the alcoholic, it is the beginning of a love affair. In the beginning, drinking brings feelings of warmth, goodwill and a sense of harmony to the inner life of an alcoholic.

"The majority of those who become addicted are people with a mystical streak, an appetite for inexhaustible bliss," states Tom P. Jr., in Gresham's Law and Alcoholics Anonymous.

A PROGRESSIVE DISEASE

Drinking becomes the focal point, the hub, in an alcoholic's wheel of life. Decisions, courses of action, activities, social affiliations, family life and choices of employment are the spokes of the wheel. Over time, the negative consequences of drinking may become apparent, by those personally associated with the alcoholic to the society at large, that drinking is the cause of the problems. However, in the mind of the alcoholic, drinking has become the solution to the mounting problems in his life.

Even when the alcoholic can no longer deny the relationship between the negative consequences in his life to his drinking, he will continue to drink. The man takes a drink, the drink takes a drink, the drink takes the man. In the Big Book of Alcoholics Anonymous, alcoholism is defined as a baffling, cunning disease. Bert Pluymen, author of The Thinking Person's Guide To Sobriety explains it this way: "And the greatest difficulty is that it's not the elbow or kneecap that becomes addicted but the brain. The very organ that likes alcohol is making the decision on whether to change the behavior. Guess what it will always decide?"

THE PREVALENCE OF PROBLEM DRINKING

Alcohol is the most widely used psychoactive drug in the United States and nearly 13.8 million Americans 18 years and older have problems with drinking. It is estimated that one-fourth of all persons admitted to general hospitals have alcohol problems or are undiagnosed alcoholics being treated for the consequences of their drinking. Heavy and chronic drinking can harm every organ and system in the body and it is the third leading cause of preventable mortality. Alcohol is involved in almost half of all homicides and serious assaults, sex-related crimes, robberies and domestic violence. Approximately 42 percent of adults have been exposed to alcoholism in the family and one in five children live in a home with an alcoholic parent.

GENETIC FACTORS

Alcoholism is being studied and discussed within the nurture vs. nature context. Parents' positive attitudes and behaviors in relation to drinking, lack of parental involvement, harsh and inconsistent discipline or hostility and rejection experienced by a child can predict future alcohol abuse for the child in adolescence and adulthood. A low brain wave, P300, responding to specific light or sound stimuli, is a proven indicator of an increased risk of alcoholism and drug abuse in the sons of alco-

---

A WIDESPREAD PROBLEM

For most people, alcohol is a pleasant accompaniment to social activities. Moderate alcohol use—up to two drinks per day for men and one drink per day for women and older people (A standard drink is one 12-ounce bottle of beer or wine cooler, one 5-ounce glass of wine, or 1.5 ounces of 80-proof distilled spirits)—is not harmful for most adults. Nonetheless, a substantial number of people have serious trouble with their drinking. Currently, nearly 14 million Americans—1 in every 13 adults—abuse alcohol or are alcoholic. Several million more adults engage in risky drinking patterns that could lead to alcohol problems. In addition, approximately 53 percent of men and women in the United States report that one or more of their close relatives have a drinking problem.

The consequences of alcohol misuse are serious—in many cases, life-threatening. Heavy drinking can increase the risk for certain cancers, especially those of the liver, esophagus, throat, and larynx (voice box). It can also cause liver cirrhosis, immune system problems, brain damage, and harm to the fetus during pregnancy. In addition, drinking increases the risk of death from automobile crashes, recreational accidents, and on-the-job accidents and also increases the likelihood of homicide and suicide. In purely economic terms, alcohol-use problems cost society approximately $100 billion per year. In human terms, the costs are incalculable.

National Institute on Alcohol Abuse and Alcoholism, *Alcoholism: Getting the Facts,* November 1996.

---

holics. Genetic mapping has identified specific genes involved in the adaptation of the brain to alcohol affecting behavioral and biological responses that differ in the alcoholic from the non-alcoholic drinker.

Dispelling the myth that alcoholism is the bad habit of a morally weak and over-indulgent person, research studies have proven alcoholism has its roots in genetic susceptibility, social circumstance and personal behavior causing inescapable cravings and compulsive use due to the biochemical and structural changes in the brain of a person genetically predisposed to addiction.

| "The large majority of problem drinkers outgrow their drinking problems."

THE DANGERS OF ALCOHOL ABUSE ARE EXAGGERATED

Stanton Peele

In the following viewpoint, Stanton Peele challenges common assumptions about alcoholism. He maintains that alcoholics have control over their drinking and usually stop drinking of their own volition. Furthermore, the majority of alcohol abusers are college-age men who outgrow their drinking problems as they mature. Peele, who writes frequently about the subject of addiction, is the author of *Diseasing of America*, from which the following viewpoint is excerpted.

As you read, consider the following questions:

1. What evidence does Peele provide to support his assertion that alcoholics can control their drinking?
2. As defined by the author, what is alcoholic progression?
3. As cited by Peele, what research studies support the view that most alcoholics outgrow their drinking problems?

The core idea of the Alcoholics Anonymous (AA) version of the disease of alcoholism is that alcoholics cannot cease drinking once they start. The first step of AA, admitting that the alcoholic is "powerless over alcohol," means that alcoholics simply cannot regulate their drinking in any way. According to AA, even a single taste of alcohol (such as that in an alcoholic dessert) sets off uncontrollable binge drinking. Alcoholism professionals have attempted to translate AA's view into scientific-sounding terms. For example, in a popular book on alcoholism, Under the Influence, James Milam claims: "The alcoholic's drinking is controlled by physiological factors which cannot be altered through psychological methods such as counseling, threats, punishment, or reward. In other words, the alcoholic is powerless to control his or her drinking."[1]

In fact, this statement has been demonstrated to be false by every experiment designed to test it. For example, alcoholics who are not aware that they are drinking alcohol do not develop an uncontrollable urge to drink more.[2] Psychologist Alan Marlatt and his colleagues found that alcoholics drinking heavily flavored alcoholic beverages did not drink excessive amounts—as long as they thought the drinks did not contain alcohol. The alcoholics in this experiment who drank the most were those who believed they were imbibing alcohol—*even when their beverage contained none*.[3] From this study, we see that what alcoholics believe is more important to their drinking than the "facts" that they are alcoholics and that they are drinking alcohol.

ALCOHOLICS HAVE CONTROL OVER THEIR DRINKING

Rather than losing control of their drinking, experiments show, alcoholics aim for a desired state of consciousness when they drink.[4] They drink to transform their emotions and their self-image—drinking is a route to achieve feelings of power, sexual attractiveness, or control over unpleasant emotions.[5] Alcoholics strive to attain a particular level of intoxication, one that they can describe before taking a drink. Nancy Mello and Jack Mendelson of Harvard Medical School and McLean Hospital—the former a psychologist and the latter a physician—found that alcoholics would continue working to gain credits with which to buy alcohol until they could stockpile the amount they needed to get as drunk as they wanted. They continued to work for credits as they were undergoing withdrawal from previous binges, even though they could stop and turn in their credits for drink at any time.[6]

Alcoholics are influenced by their environments and by those around them, even when they are drinking and intoxicated. For example, researchers at Baltimore City Hospital offered alcoholics the opportunity to drink whenever they wanted in a small, drab isolation booth. These street inebriates curtailed their drinking significantly in order to spend more time in a comfortable and interesting room among their companions. In these and other studies, alcoholics' drinking behavior was molded simply by the way the alcohol was administered or by the rewards alcoholics received or were denied based on their drinking styles.[7]

What does this research prove? *Alcoholism* is the term we use to describe people who get drunk more than other people and who often suffer problems due to their drinking. Alcoholism exists—overdrinking, compulsive drinking, drinking beyond a point where the person knows he or she will regret it—all these occur. (In fact, these things happen to quite a high percentage of all drinkers during their lives.) But this drinking is not due to some special, uncontrollable biological drive. Alcoholics are no different from other human beings in exercising choices, in seeking the feelings that they believe alcohol provides, and in evaluating the mood changes they experience in terms of their alternatives. No evidence disputes the view that alcoholics continue to respond to their environments and to express personal values even while they are drinking. . . .

THE MYTH OF ALCOHOLIC PROGRESSION

The nineteenth-century view of alcoholic progression—that occasional drinkers become regular drinkers become alcoholics—is alive and well in the modern alcoholism movement. Now the idea is that anyone who ever has any problems with their drinking must either seek treatment or progress to inevitable, life-threatening alcoholism. "The ultimate consequences for a drinking alcoholic," Dr. G. Douglas Talbott says, "are these three: he or she will end up in jail, in a hospital, or in a graveyard."[8]

Of course, when you talk to alcoholics, you discover that they were early problem drinkers before they progressed to alcoholism. But the fact is, the large majority of problem drinkers outgrow their drinking problems, according to the national surveys conducted by Don Cahalan and his associates. Men often go through problem drinking periods, depending on their stage in the life cycle and the people they associate with, only to emerge from these when their life circumstances change. Incidentally, the large majority of these untreated former problem drinkers do not choose to abstain but continue drinking while diminish-

The push to cut alcohol consumption is built on the belief that some 10 percent of American adults have what are called "drinking problems"—a figure that, like every statistic associated with alcohol, is questioned by specialists.

Researcher Joseph E. Josephson, writing in a publication for the Columbia University School of Public Health, has questioned the very idea that there is a large number of problem drinkers in America: "An objective assessment of government statistics on alcohol-related problems, many of them compiled in the Third Report to the U.S. Congress on Alcohol and Health in 1978, indicates that there is little sound basis for claims that there are upwards of 10 million problem drinkers (including alcoholics) in the adult population and that their number is increasing; that there are 1.5 to 2.25 million problem drinkers among women; that there are over 3 million problem drinkers among youth; that the heavy consumption of alcohol by pregnant women leads consistently to a cluster of birth defects . . . [and] that half of all motor vehicle accident fatalities are alcohol-related. . . . These and other claims about the extent and consequences of alcohol use and abuse—some of them fanciful, others as yet to be supported by research—are part of the 'numbers game' which besets discussion of alcohol-related problems and policy."

Dave Shiflett, *American Spectator*, October 1996.

---

ing or eliminating their problems. The largest group of problem drinkers is young men, but young drinkers show the highest rate of natural remission as they age.[9]

Several surveys conducted by Kaye Fillmore, of the Institute for Health and Aging (University of California, San Francisco), indicate that drinking problems that appear in college and late adolescence—problems up to and including blackout—*rarely* persist through middle age.[10] Exactly similar data pertain to youthful drug abuse, and all research shows the tendency to use, to use regularly, and to be addicted to drugs drops off after adolescence and early adulthood.[11] Apparently, as people mature they find they can achieve more meaningful rewards than those offered by drugs and overdrinking. These rewards are generally the conventional ones of family life and accomplishment at work that dominate adult life for most people, even most of those who had a drinking or drug problem earlier on.

Nor are children of alcoholics destined to progress to alcoholism when they drink. A large, long-term study of Tecumseh, Michigan, residents conducted by epidemiologists at the University of Michigan found that children of heavy-drinking parents most frequently choose to drink moderately themselves. Although alcoholics have more alcoholic offspring than average, the researchers noted, "alcoholic parental drinking only weakly invites imitation."[12] It seems that people are quite capable of learning from observing a parent's alcoholism to avoid such problems themselves. In doing so, the researchers found, children are helped when the heavy drinker is the parent of the opposite sex. In addition, there was *less* imitation in this study of a heavy-drinking parent when the children as adults recalled the parent as having drinking problems.[13] Finally, several studies of children of alcoholics have shown that, even after they themselves develop a drinking problem, they do better in treatment aimed at moderating drinking rather than at abstinence than do other problem drinkers.[14]

SELF-CURE AMONG ALCOHOLICS

Although by far the largest percentage of those who outgrow a drinking or drug problem without treatment are younger, natural recovery in alcoholism and addiction is not limited to the young or to those who fall short of developing severe alcoholism.[15] Those who have progressed to definite alcohol dependence also regularly escape from alcoholism on their own; indeed, natural remission for alcoholics may be more typical than not. In the words of British physician Milton Gross, who has focused on the biological aspects of alcohol dependence:

> The foundation is set for the progression of the alcohol dependence syndrome by virtue of its biologically intensifying itself. One would think that, once caught up in the process, the individual could not be extricated. However, and for reasons poorly understood, the reality is otherwise. Many, perhaps most, do free themselves.[16]

A number of studies have now documented that such self-cure among alcoholics is common. These untreated but recovered alcoholics constitute, according to researcher Barry Tuchfeld, a "silent majority."[17] Based on his research in Australia, psychiatrist Les Drew has described alcoholism as a "self-limiting" disease, one that creates pressures for its own cure even in the absence of outside interventions.[18] In the words of Harold Mulford, "Contrary to the traditional clinical view of the alcoholism disease process, progress in the alcoholic process is neither inevitable nor irreversible. Eventually, the balance of natural forces shifts to decelerate progress in the alcoholic process and to accelerate the rehabilitation process."[19]

Notes can be found on page 186.

Periodical Bibliography

The following articles have been selected to supplement the diverse views presented in this chapter. Addresses are provided for periodicals not indexed in the *Readers' Guide to Periodical Literature*, the *Alternative Press Index*, the *Social Sciences Index*, or the *Index to Legal Periodicals and Books*.

George Bain	"A Phoney Debate over Cigarette Addiction," *Maclean's*, August 26, 1996.
Ralph Hyatt	"Sex Addiction," *USA Today*, November 1997.
Mike Males and Faye Docuyanan	"The Return of Reefer Madness: Exaggerated Reports of Teenage Drug Use," *Progressive*, May 1, 1996.
Debi Martin-Morris	"Teens on Heroin," *Teen*, October 1997.
Anne Platt McGinn	"The Nicotine Cartel," *World Watch*, July/August 1997.
Mark Nichols	"Is Sex an Addiction?" *Maclean's*, February 9, 1998.
Ronald A. Reno	"The Diceman Cometh," *Policy Review*, March/April 1996.
Debbie Seaman	"Hooked Online," *Time*, October 12, 1998.
Jan Marie Werblin	"Addiction in the Golden Years," *Professional Counselor*, October 1998. Available from PO Box 420235, Palm Coast, FL 32142-0235.

CHAPTER 3

HOW SHOULD
ADDICTION
BE TREATED?

CHAPTER PREFACE

The goal of most treatment programs is to get addicts off drugs—and to keep them that way. Disagreement persists over whether treatment programs have lasting results, with critics pointing out that even addicts who desperately want to quit often relapse. Even more difficult is the challenge of treating drug addicts who do not wish to quit. Heroin addicts, for example, often resist treatment because they fear the excruciating withdrawal symptoms that come with quitting heroin.

One response to the difficulty of treating resistant addicts is harm reduction programs—programs that aim to reduce the social costs of drug addiction, such as crime and the spread of disease through shared needles. The most widely implemented harm reduction measure is needle exchange programs, which allow addicts to trade used syringes for clean ones. Another, more controversial approach involves administering legal, low-cost heroin, cocaine, and other drugs to addicts in a supervised medical environment as a way of preventing drug-related crime.

The underlying philosophy behind harm reduction is that some drug use in society is inevitable. Therefore, treatment programs should strive to minimize the effects of addiction on society—not eliminate drug use entirely. Proponents believe harm reduction is a step toward a better life for addicts and a better society in general. According to Robert W. Westermeyer, "The harm reduction model upholds that any movement toward improved well being and reduced harm is positive in and of itself."

To its critics, however, harm reduction is nothing more than the perpetuation of addiction. Drug czar Barry McCaffrey calls harm reduction "a half-way measure, a half-hearted approach [to drug addiction]." According to McCaffrey, "Alcohol is no help for alcoholism [and] heroin is no cure for heroin addiction."

Many new treatment programs, from methadone maintenance programs to proposals that alcoholics can learn to drink in moderation, are guided by the principles of harm reduction. The following chapter discusses the advantages and disadvantages of these and other methods of treating addiction.

"Through treatment that is tailored
to individual needs, patients can
learn to control their [addiction]
and live normal, productive lives."

TREATMENT PROGRAMS HELP ADDICTS RECOVER

National Institute on Drug Abuse

The National Institute on Drug Abuse (NIDA), a federal agency established in 1974 to research the health aspects of drug abuse and addiction, maintains in the following viewpoint that rehabilitation programs are effective in treating drug or alcohol addiction. The four most common types of treatment programs—outpatient treatment, therapeutic communities, short-term residential treatment, and methadone maintenance programs—all have high rates of success.

As you read, consider the following questions:

1. What evidence does NIDA provide to support the effectiveness of treatment programs?
2. How do drug treatment programs impact crime rates, according to NIDA?
3. In NIDA's view, why are treatment programs cost-effective?

Reprinted from "Treatment Methods," NIDA Infofax, February 11, 1998, at www.nida.nih.gov/infofax/treatmeth.html.

Drug addiction is a treatable disorder. Through treatment that is tailored to individual needs, patients can learn to control their condition and live normal, productive lives. Like people with diabetes or heart disease, people in treatment for drug addiction learn behavioral changes and often take medications as part of their treatment regimen.

Behavioral therapies can include counseling, psychotherapy, support groups, or family therapy. Treatment medications offer help in suppressing the withdrawal syndrome and drug craving and in blocking the effects of drugs. In addition, studies show that treatment for heroin addiction using methadone at an adequate dosage level combined with behavioral therapy reduces death rates and many health problems associated with heroin abuse.

In general, the more treatment given, the better the results. Many patients require other services as well, such as medical and mental health services and HIV prevention services. Patients who stay in treatment longer than 3 months usually have better outcomes than those who stay less time. Patients who go through medically assisted withdrawal to minimize discomfort but do not receive any further treatment perform about the same in terms of their drug use as those who were never treated. Various studies have shown that treatment works to reduce drug intake and crimes committed by drug-dependent people. Researchers also have found that drug abusers who have been through treatment are more likely to have jobs.

THE GOALS OF TREATMENT

The ultimate goal of all drug abuse treatment is to enable the patient to achieve lasting abstinence, but the immediate goals are to reduce drug use, improve the patient's ability to function, and minimize the medical and social complications of drug abuse.

There are several types of drug abuse treatment programs. Short-term methods last less than 6 months and include residential therapy, medication therapy, and drug-free outpatient therapy. Longer term treatment may include, for example, methadone maintenance outpatient treatment for opiate addicts and residential therapeutic community treatment.

HOW ADDICTION TREATMENT WORKS

In maintenance treatment for heroin addicts, people in treatment are given an oral dose of a synthetic opiate, usually methadone hydrochloride or levo-alpha-acetyl methadol (LAAM), administered at a dosage sufficient to block the effects of heroin and yield a stable, noneuphoric state free from physiological craving for opiates. In this stable state, the patient is able to disengage from drug-seeking and related criminal behavior and, with appropriate counseling and social services, become a productive member of his or her community.

Outpatient drug-free treatment does not include medications and encompasses a wide variety of programs for patients who visit a clinic at regular intervals. Most of the programs involve individual or group counseling. Patients entering these programs are abusers of drugs other than opiates or are opiate abusers for whom maintenance therapy is not recommended, such as those who have stable, well-integrated lives and only brief histories of drug dependence.

Therapeutic communities (TCs) are highly structured programs in which patients stay at a residence, typically for 6 to 12 months. Patients in TCs include those with relatively long histories of drug dependence, involvement in serious criminal activities, and seriously impaired social functioning. The focus of the TC is on the resocialization of the patient to a drug-free, crime-free lifestyle.

Short-term residential programs, often referred to as chemical dependency units, are often based on the "Minnesota Model" of treatment for alcoholism. These programs involve a 3- to 6-week inpatient treatment phase followed by extended outpatient therapy or participation in 12-step self-help groups, such as Narcotics Anonymous or Cocaine Anonymous. Chemical dependency programs for drug abuse arose in the private sector in the mid-1980s with insured alcohol/cocaine abusers as their primary patients. Today, as private provider benefits decline, more programs are extending their services to publicly funded patients.

Methadone maintenance programs are usually more successful at retaining clients with opiate dependence than are therapeutic communities, which in turn are more successful than outpatient programs that provide psychotherapy and counseling. Within various methadone programs, those that provide higher doses of methadone (usually a minimum of 60 mg.) have better retention rates. Also, those that provide other services, such as counseling, therapy, and medical care, along with methadone generally get better results than the programs that provide minimal services.

DRUG TREATMENT IN PRISONS

Drug treatment programs in prisons can succeed in preventing patients' return to criminal behavior, particularly if they are linked to community-based programs that continue treatment when the

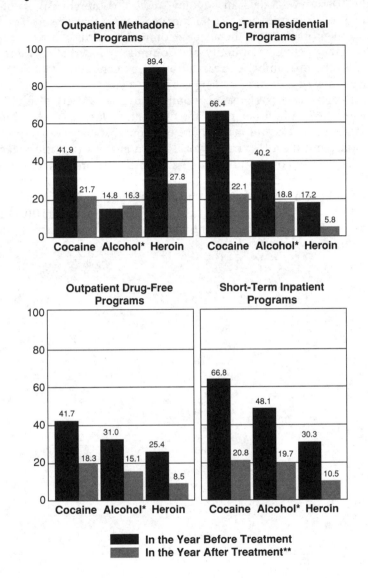

* Weekly or more frequent use with 5 or more drinks at a sitting.
** Outpatient methadone patients still in treatment were interviewed
approximately 24 months after admission.

Michael D. Mueller and June R. Wyman, NIDA Notes, September/October 1997.

client leaves prison. Some of the more successful programs have reduced the rearrest rate by one-fourth to one-half. For example, the "Delaware Model," an ongoing study of comprehensive treatment of drug-addicted prison inmates, shows that prison-based treatment including a therapeutic community setting, a work release therapeutic community, and community-based aftercare reduces the probability of rearrest by 57 percent and reduces the likelihood of returning to drug use by 37 percent.

Drug abuse has a great economic impact on society—an estimated $67 billion per year. This figure includes costs related to crime, medical care, drug abuse treatment, social welfare programs, and time lost from work. Treatment of drug abuse can reduce those costs. Studies have shown that from $4 to $7 are saved for every dollar spent on treatment. It costs approximately $3,600 per month to leave a drug abuser untreated in the community, and incarceration costs approximately $3,300 per month. In contrast, methadone maintenance therapy costs about $290 per month.

"Research suggests that most people
who have problems with both licit
and illicit substances don't seek
treatment, and many manage to
resolve their problems by themselves."

MANY ADDICTS RECOVER WITHOUT TREATMENT

Anita Dubey

In the following viewpoint, Anita Dubey attests that many
people overcome substance use problems without treatment.
Research demonstrates that addicts who are motivated to quit
and possess strong social support systems are able to recover
without professional help. Dubey is the editor of The Journal, an
Ontario-based publication for addiction specialists.

As you read, consider the following questions:

1. According to Dubey, what research studies demonstrate the
   effectiveness of spontaneous recovery?
2. For what reasons do people resist treatment programs, in
   Dubey's view?
3. What are some characteristics of addicts who recover without
   professional help?

Adapted from Anita Dubey, "Recovering Naturally," The Journal, November/December
1996, by permission of the author.

The basic reason I quit was because I had to. I thought it was going to kill me really soon. I was so paranoid of being caught with cocaine that I would sit in my house in the dark with a flashlight, so nobody knew I was home, and draw my lines. It was getting to the point where I'd been selling my things to support my habit. But I couldn't see myself stealing. So I moved to a different town, and I quit.—Jack

On the surface, Jack might seem like a candidate for a treatment program. His daily amphetamine habit had turned into an addiction to injecting cocaine, and by the age of 38, he had been abusing drugs for nine years. During that time, Jack maintained the trappings of a middle-class life, holding a steady job and owning a home in a small city in Wyoming.

But Jack never sought professional help. After making the decision to stop using drugs, he did so on his own.

Research suggests that most people who have problems with both licit and illicit substances don't seek treatment, and many manage to resolve their problems by themselves. It questions the idea that treatment, formal interventions or self-help groups are the only way to help someone with substance use problems.

"There is a history of making the mistake of exaggerating the threat of drugs' effects," says Lee Robins, a psychiatrist at St. Louis University in Missouri. More than 20 years ago, Robins found that most Vietnam veterans who had become addicted to heroin in the war recovered without any treatment on their return to the United States.

"Drug use can be dangerous, but there is a fairly high rate of spontaneous recovery," she says. "I think it's important that people know that it happens."

Studies on Spontaneous Recovery

In one recent study, 78 per cent of people who had reported at least one alcohol-related problem in the past reduced or quit drinking on their own. Subjects had to be recovered for a minimum of one year in the study by researchers at the Addiction Research Foundation (ARF) and Nova Southeastern University in Fort Lauderdale, Florida.

The study, which was published in *American Journal of Public Health*, looked at data from two surveys, the 1989 *National Alcohol and Drugs Survey* with 11,634 subjects, and the 1993 *Ontario Alcohol and Drug Opinion Survey* with 1,034 subjects. An unpublished analysis of data from the 1994 *Canadian Alcohol and Drug Survey* found a rate of 82 per cent.

"This simply shows there are multiple pathways to recovery," said Linda Sobell, formerly senior scientist at the ARF, who is currently with Nova Southeastern University.

Researchers say that identifying the strategies that this under-studied population uses could benefit anyone with a substance problem. It can help design better treatment programs, and find triggers to help people outside the treatment system.

HELPING ADDICTS WHO REJECT TRADITIONAL TREATMENT

"There are many individuals with problems who will never access traditional treatment," said John Cunningham, an ARF scientist who co-authored the study. "We need to be thinking about how to help those individuals.". . .

Any number of factors may keep people out of treatment: stigma, pride, disdain of treatment programs, a desire to solve the problem themselves, a feeling the problem is not so serious it needs professional help.

The area of help-seeking behaviors is, however, one that needs more research, says Jalie Tucker, a psychologist at Auburn University in Alabama. "The treatment-outcome research agenda has dominated the field."

What is better known is that the problems that motivate people to quit on their own are similar to those that motivate others to quit with the help of treatment. Poor health is one of the main factors cited in studies of both alcohol and illicit drugs, but family problems and the realization of how damaging substance abuse is also play a role.

However, the literature suggests that, for alcohol abuse at least, there is no single event that triggers a decision to quit, but rather a combination of influences.

THE IMPORTANCE OF SOCIAL SUPPORT NETWORKS

A key factor that seems to help people initiate and maintain recovery on their own is having social support networks, says Bob Granfield, a sociologist at the University of Denver in Colorado. Granfield co-authored a qualitative study, published in the *Journal of Drug Issues*, of 46 middle-class people who had overcome an alcohol or other drug addiction.

They found that former users "got out of places where their drug-using networks were," says Granfield. They abandoned drug-using communities, and some even moved to different cities. Relying heavily on family and friends, they reintegrated themselves into more conventional networks, joining clubs or churches and taking up new leisure pursuits.

"A lot of people found God," he says. "That's not unlike AA

[Alcoholics Anonymous] or other self-help groups."

Robins says that the Vietnam vets simply weren't expecting to stay addicted. "When they got home, they felt they had to clean up their act or their girlfriends or mothers wouldn't like it."

Several studies have noted the importance of family and other social relations in natural recovery. Half of the "natural recoverers" in an Alabama study of resolved drinkers cited the role of family members in helping them stay clean. Such support was more influential in natural recoveries than in recoveries associated with treatment or AA participation. Recovered problem drinkers who had received interventions were more likely to mention AA—with its social network supporting abstinence—as their main source of help. The study, by Tucker and colleagues, was published in *Experimental and Clinical Psychopharmacology*. . . .

CHARACTERISTICS OF PEOPLE WHO RECOVER WITHOUT TREATMENT

Some characteristics are known about people who do recover on their own.

Generally, people with more severe problems are more likely to end up in treatment. In the Canadian national study, subjects who had received treatment reported an average of 3.6 past alcohol-related problems on a scale of five. This compares with a figure of two past problems among people who were abstinent and had not received treatment. Meanwhile, people who had recovered to drink moderately without treatment had an average of just 1.5 past problems.

The survey also found the latter group was from a higher socioeconomic status, and had higher incomes and more education than the abstinent group.

Similarly, a California survey of drinkers who recovered without treatment found that the group drinking moderately had fewer prior symptoms of dependence, and fewer drinking-related problems and health problems than the abstinent group. They also had better social networks, more social support and greater confidence that they could resist drinking.

The results highlight the fact that, even among those who recover on their own, there is a range of backgrounds, problems and resolutions. . . .

"The treatment world has a universal definition for addiction," says Granfield. "That may not be what's needed." Most subjects in the Denver study did not identify with the "addict" identity, although they had been dependent on alcohol or other drugs for an average of nine years. Most did not even classify themselves as even a "recovered addict."

Some researchers have suggested there needs to be a shift toward looking at substance abuse as often a temporary phase in a person's life.

Another piece of the puzzle left is to figure out how to reach people who are reluctant to go to treatment, or who don't have the resources to, says Granfield. One idea is to simply publicize the notion that it is possible to get over an addiction without treatment, by taking advantage of users' networks.

PROMOTING NATURAL RECOVERY FROM DRINKING PROBLEMS

Sobell and Cunningham are working with ARF colleagues on a new study to promote change in people concerned about their drinking, who don't necessarily want treatment. "If we can get to the problem earlier, we can reduce the costs to the individual, and to society," says Sobell.

Using newspaper ads, the researchers aim to recruit about 800 people. The study will evaluate the effectiveness of different mailed-out materials in helping people deal with their alcohol problems without treatment. Subjects will be followed up for a year in the Fostering Self-Change project, which is funded by the U.S. National Institute on Alcohol Abuse and Alcoholism.

"What we're doing is providing the minimally-required intervention," Sobell says.

The success of a book that helped people to reduce their alcohol consumption points to the impact that non-formal treatment interventions can have.

A study of people who read the book *Saying When: How to Quit*

Drinking or Cut Down by former ARF researcher Martha Sanchez-Craig found that, one year after reading the book, subjects had reduced their drinking by one-half and more than 60 per cent were drinking moderately within recommended guidelines. The book was targeted at people whose drinking was starting to interfere with their lives, rather than those with a severe problem.

Although the field is moving toward different types of treatment, such as brief or minimal intervention, there still is a need for more heterogeneous programs, Tucker says.

"There are different interventions for different people," agrees Sobell. "If someone has high blood pressure, exercise and a better diet works for some people, but not everyone. The same applies to [substance use] problems."

| "Medical- and alcohol-treatment communities in the United States [have applied] to all drinkers the advice appropriate for the most severely afflicted: abstinence."

PROBLEM DRINKERS CAN LEARN MODERATION

Nancy Shute and Laura Tangley

In the following viewpoint, Nancy Shute and Laura Tangley explain a new approach to alcoholism: programs that teach problem drinkers how to moderate their consumption of alcohol. According to the authors, many problem drinkers can modify their drinking habits instead of giving up alcohol entirely. Shute and Tangley are reporters for *U.S. News & World Report* magazine.

As you read, consider the following questions:

1. What is the distinction between a problem drinker and an alcoholic, in Shute and Tangley's view?
2. What advice do most treatment programs apply to all problem drinkers, according to the authors?
3. What evidence do the authors provide to support the effectiveness of brief intervention programs aimed at helping people to moderate their drinking?

There are 40 million problem drinkers in the United States—people whose drinking causes economic, physical, or family harm but who are not technically alcoholic (defined as being physiologically dependent on alcohol). Since Prohibition was repealed in 1933, treatment for drinking problems in this country has focused almost exclusively on alcoholics, has offered abstinence as the sole cure for their problems, and has laid just two paths to that cure: Alcoholics Anonymous (AA), the spiritual self-help group founded in 1935; and a variety of related 12-step programs, originally developed at the Hazelden Foundation and other Minnesota clinics in the 1950s, which combine psychological and peer counseling and AA attendance. (AA is the granddaddy of 12-step programs, but the two approaches are not synonymous. AA is a self-help group aimed at sobriety and spiritual renewal; 12-step alcohol-treatment programs adopt some of AA's tenets but include a wide array of secular treatments, from psychotherapy to acupuncture.)

A . . . reporter, querying a dozen treatment centers about her options as someone concerned about her drinking, was offered only abstinence-based programs. The Mayo Clinic told her she was welcome to try cutting back on her own and then to come back if she failed. At the Betty Ford Center, a kindly woman answering the phone said, "For people like us, one drink always leads to another. You may be functional now, but it's progressive."

The problem with that advice is that for many people it's not true. For at least the past decade, researchers have known that the majority of people who drink heavily don't become alcoholics; some experts place that number as high as 75 percent. Other drinkers may meet the clinical criteria for alcohol dependence but can sustain controlled drinking for months, even years, before getting into trouble. And the majority of people who cut back or quit drinking do so on their own. Many of those people binge drank in their 20s at college parties, at after-work happy hours, or during Sunday afternoon football games, then got a good job, got married, got busy, and lost interest in getting smashed. In the researchers' lingo, they "matured out."

THE COSTS OF PROBLEM DRINKING

Moreover, alcoholism cannot be blamed for the majority of social ills linked to drinking in this country. Misuse of alcohol costs the nation dearly—$100 billion a year in quantifiable costs, in addition to untold emotional pain. Yet the bulk of these costs are incurred not by alcoholics but by problem drinkers, who are four times more numerous than alcoholics, are more active in society, and usually reject abstinence as a solution. Alcohol figures in 41 percent of traffic crash fatalities and is a factor in 50 percent of homicides, 30 percent of suicides, and 30 percent of accidental deaths. (In 1997, a 20-year-old Louisiana State University student drank himself to death during fraternity pledge week; three other students were hospitalized.) Heavy drinking also increases the risk of cancer, heart disease, and stroke, long before people have to worry about cirrhosis of the liver, brain damage, or other skid-row ailments. A 1990 report by the Institute of Medicine, an arm of the National Academy of Sciences, concluded that the harmful consequences of alcohol could not be reduced significantly unless more options were offered to people with only "mild to moderate" alcohol problems.

Public-health experts recognized the social costs of alcohol abuse long ago and have responded with programs such as free soft drinks for designated drivers and free taxi rides home on New Year's Eve. But because of deeply held beliefs in the American alcohol-treatment community, this kind of pragmatic, public-health-centered approach has rarely been applied to individuals with drinking problems. Europe, Great Britain, and Australia long ago defined problem drinking as a public-health concern and have established controlled-drinking programs to reduce its physical harm and social costs. Forty-three percent of Canadian treatment programs deem moderate drinking acceptable for some clients.

But in the United States, researchers and counselors who have championed—or even tried to investigate—moderation as a treatment strategy have been threatened, sometimes fired. "We've been accused of murder. That we're all in denial. That we're enablers," says Alan Marlatt, a professor of psychology and moderate-drinking proponent who is director of the University of Washington's Addictive Behaviors Research Center.

DRAWING A LINE BETWEEN ALCOHOLISM AND PROBLEM DRINKING

A big part of the problem is that it's hard to draw a clear line between alcohol dependency and problem drinking. According to a 1996 report by the University of Connecticut's Alcohol Research Center, 20 percent of American adults are problem drinkers, compared with 5 percent who are alcohol dependent. The National Institute on Alcohol Abuse and Alcoholism (NIAAA), using much stricter criteria, puts the numbers at 3 percent alcohol abusers, 1.7 percent alcohol dependents, and 2.7 percent drinkers who exhibit characteristics of both. (Discrepancies in alcohol statistics abound.)

Briefly put, problem drinkers are people who have had problems because of drinking (a DUI arrest, marital discord, showing up late to work). But they usually don't drink steadily and don't go through withdrawal when they stop. By contrast, someone who is alcohol dependent (the medically preferred term for alcoholic) exhibits at least three of the following symptoms: tolerance; withdrawal; an inability to cut down; sacrificing work, family, or social events to drink; devoting a lot of time to finding and consuming alcohol; or persistence in drinking despite related health problems.

Even so, the distinctions leave plenty of diagnostic wiggle room. The medical- and alcohol-treatment communities in the United States have dealt with this ambiguity by applying to all drinkers the advice appropriate for the most severely afflicted.

How To Manage Moderation

The moderate drinking limit is a blood alcohol level of .055 percent. For most people, moderate drinking guidelines recommend a daily limit of three drinks for women and four drinks for men. The following chart shows how this amount of alcohol will affect blood alcohol concentrations.

Women: Blood Alcohol Concentrations after Three Drinks*

Weight (lbs.)		110	120	130	140	150	160	170	180
Number	1	.126	.114	.104	.095	.088	.081	.076	.071
of	2	.110	.098	.088	.079	.072	.065	.060	.055
hours	3	.094	.082	.072	.063	.056	.049	.044	.039
	4	.078	.066	.056	.047	.040	.033	.028	.023

Men: Blood Alcohol Concentrations after Four Drinks*

Weight (lbs.)		140	150	160	170	180	190	200	210
Number	1	.108	.099	.092	.086	.080	.075	.071	.066
of	2	.092	.083	.076	.070	.064	.059	.055	.050
hours	3	.076	.067	.060	.057	.048	.043	.039	.034
	4	.060	.051	.044	.038	.032	.027	.023	.018

*A standard drink equals one 12-ounce beer, one 5-ounce glass of wine, or one and a half ounces of 80-proof liquor.

Audrey Kishline, *Psychology Today*, January/February 1996.

abstinence. Any other strategy, they feel, is too risky. "Every alcoholic would like to drink moderately," says Douglas Talbott, a physician and president of the American Society of Addiction Medicine. "Ninety percent have tried. This just feeds into the denial of the alcoholic."

Moderate-drinking proponents concede that some alcoholics will seize upon controlled drinking as an excuse to avoid abstinence. But they say that they explicitly warn that the strategy is not for alcoholics, only for people with less severe drinking problems; that tests can evaluate the intensity of difficulties; and that they regularly refer dependent drinkers to AA. Controlled drinking, says Marc Kern, a Los Angeles psychologist, can "reduce harm by reducing alcohol consumption" and can propel people who fail at moderation into abstinence.

THE ORIGINS OF TEMPERANCE

America's ambivalence toward alcohol is long standing. In the early days of the republic, we were a nation of lushes. Per capita consumption of alcohol was three times today's. The first temperance effort, led by Philadelphia physician Benjamin Rush in the 1780s, prescribed moderation: Rush urged people to switch from rum and gin to the more salubrious beer and wine.

Temperance soon moved from the doctor's office to the church. In 1826, the Rev. Lyman Beecher galvanized the movement with his Six Sermons on Intemperance, which held that alcohol was a poison and that abstinence was the only answer. "This is the way to death!" Beecher said of the drinking life. Ever since, the nature of alcohol abuse has been debated, the arguments often mixing the medical and the moral. Is it a bad habit, a matter of will, or a disease?

THE DISEASE CONCEPT OF ALCOHOLISM

The medical model that has dominated alcohol treatment for more than a half century holds that alcohol dependence is an ailment with biological and genetic roots. Research suggests there is a genetic predisposition toward alcoholism; identical twins, for instance, are more apt to share a drinking problem than fraternal twins, and adopted children whose birth parents were alcoholics are four times likelier than children adopted from nonalcoholic homes to become alcohol dependent. This disease approach is challenged by behaviorists, the primary advocates of controlled drinking, who say alcohol abuse is a behavior influenced by psychological, cultural, and environmental forces, not just physiology.

Science has yet to come up with enough information to resolve the disease vs. behavior argument. Odds are that alcohol abuse will prove to be a combination of both, the behavioral factors dominating in problem drinkers and biological factors weighing more heavily in people who are physically addicted. But in the meantime, the disease and behavior camps have been warring as if the evidence were absolute. A 1976 Rand report saying that a very small number of alcoholics successfully moderate their drinking was fiercely attacked. "It was like desecrating the altar," says Frederick Glaser, a psychiatrist at East Carolina University School of Medicine in Greenville, N.C., who was a researcher at the time. Mark and Linda Sobell, two psychologists who in the 1970s published similar findings, were accused of faking their results and were hauled up before a congressional committee. The Sobells were later vindicated.

Though most people in the mainstream treatment community hold tightly to the disease concept of alcoholism, the treatment they offer is based on a combination of folklore and personal experience rather than on science. As Robin Room, a Canadian sociologist who is critical of American alcohol treatment, asks: "What kind of field is it that claims [alcoholism is] a disease, but the treatment is nonmedical?" Enoch Gordis, director of the NIAAA, wrote in 1987 of the nation's $3.8 billion alcohol-treatment effort: "In the case of alcoholism, our whole treatment system   is founded on hunch, not evidence, and not on science."...

Because alcohol treatment is so unscientific, some of the most basic and effective standards of care are ignored. Instead of adhering to the stepped-care protocol employed in other areas of medicine—where the least invasive treatment is used first—alcohol treatment starts with its most drastic remedy: lifetime abstinence, meetings, and, until recently, a 28-day residential stay in a substance-abuse clinic. As a result, many people who need help don't seek it. Others try AA but feel it doesn't meet their needs.

DISCOVERING MODERATION

That's what happened to Moderation Management founder Audrey Kishline. In her 20s, she was drinking five or six glasses of wine a night, drinking alone, drinking and driving. Diagnosed as an alcoholic, she was sent to detoxification, to residential treatment, and to AA. But Kishline didn't feel she had been alcohol dependent: She had no withdrawal symptoms, and she found it easy to abstain for months. She started researching alcohol treatment, and was outraged to find that alternatives common in Europe were never even mentioned here. "The public's not getting the full story," Kishline says. Now 40, married and raising two children, she occasionally has a glass of wine with dinner. Had she initially been offered less drastic treatment, Kishline believes, she would have reached this point of temperance years sooner. . . .

In April 1997, Michael Fleming, a University of Wisconsin Medical School family physician, published the first large U.S. study of brief interventions for problem drinkers in the *Journal of the American Medical Association*. The study, patterned on research over the past 20 years in Great Britain and Sweden, selected 774 problem drinkers from patients at 17 Wisconsin clinics. Half the patients met for two 15-minute sessions, one month apart, with their physicians, discussed their current health behavior and the effects of alcohol, and signed a prescription like drinking contract. A year later, the men had reduced their alcohol use by 14 percent; the women, by 30 percent. (Women are usually more successful than men at moderating.) The control group also reduced its drinking, but the brief intervention group was twice as likely to reduce it by 20 percent or more.

Other promising research is coming from Seattle, where University of Washington psychologist Marlatt is working with a notoriously immoderate population—college students. For the past seven years, he has followed 350 students who were identified while still in high school as high-risk drinkers. A year after half the students were given a one-hour, one-on-one educational session in their freshman year, 80 percent had reduced binge drinking substantially. Those who didn't were given more education and counseling, with the intensity escalating each year. "It's a harm-reduction approach," Marlatt says, using a phrase more often applied to needle exchanges and other drug-abuse programs. "With young people, if you only offer abstinence, they're not going to sign up."

Another brief intervention program, offered to adults by the University of Michigan Medical Center's DrinkWise program, is patterned on one developed at Toronto's Addiction Research Foundation. DrinkWise offers four one-hour educational counseling sessions, in person or by phone, with three- and nine-month follow-up calls, for $495. East Carolina University launched its own DrinkWise program in late 1997.

New Options for Problem Drinkers

Many people enter alcohol treatment not by choice but by court order for drunk driving and other offenses. They, too, are beginning to gain a few more options. In 1996 California ruled that Los Angeles County does not have to require offenders to attend an abstinence-based self-help group, making room for Moderation Management as a legal alternative to AA. . . .

There's reason to hope today's revolutionaries will get a more open hearing than their predecessors: The NIAAA, along with other federal agencies, is increasing funding for different alcohol treatments. Someday, perhaps, controlled-drinking programs will be as commonplace as Weight Watchers and Smokenders, and problem drinking will be recognized as a $100 billion public-health problem requiring solutions as varied and complex as our long, tempestuous relationship with alcohol.

"The only realistic goal in [the] treatment [of alcoholism] is total abstinence."

PROBLEM DRINKERS CANNOT LEARN MODERATION

Part I: Hazelden Foundation, Part II: James E. Royce

In recent years some groups have developed treatment programs aimed at teaching problem drinkers to drink in moderation. The Hazelden Foundation and James E. Royce argue in the following viewpoint that it is impossible for problem drinkers to control or modify their drinking habits. The notion that alcoholics— who by definition have lost the ability to control their alcohol consumption—can learn to drink responsibly is absurd and dangerous. In truth, the authors claim, the only successful way to cure alcohol dependency is to promote complete abstinence. The Hazelden Foundation is a nonprofit organization providing rehabilitation, education, prevention, and professional services in the field of chemical dependency. Royce, now deceased, was a Jesuit priest, professor of psychology at Seattle University, and author of *Alcoholism and Other Drug Problems*.

As you read, consider the following questions:

1. According to the Hazelden Foundation, what is the irony of alcoholics attempting to control their drinking?
2. In Royce's opinion, why is it impossible for alcoholics to learn to drink in moderation?

Part I: From "Controlled Drinking Gains Visibility but Lacks Credibility." This article was originally published in the Winter 1996 issue of the *Hazelden Voice* newsletter. Permission to reprint is granted by Hazelden Foundation, a chemical dependency treatment and education center based in Center City, Minnesota. Part II: Reprinted from James E. Royce, "Alcoholics Cannot Learn to Be 'Social Drinkers,'" *Seattle Post-Intelligencer,* July 29, 1995, by permission of the Oregon Province of the Society of Jesus.

I

Since 1949 thousands of people from all walks of life have passed through the doors of Hazelden looking for answers to their alcoholism. The majority have fought desperately to be moderate drinkers. Many have enlisted therapists from several disciplines at significant expense in this quest. In the end, a large percentage have surrendered to the idea that they cannot consistently moderate their drinking; that at times they suffer from a compulsion to drink no matter what the consequences. And finally, when they are able to look back, they are amazed at how blind they were to what was happening to them with their drinking.

Periodically, the issue of moderation management, or controlled drinking, resurfaces. It did again in 1995 when several programs gained national media attention by touting controlled drinking as an alternative to abstinence.

ALCOHOL AND THE MEDIA

To many it is unthinkable that some people cannot live a life of moderate drinking, as commonly portrayed in advertisements for alcoholic beverages. By age 14, most adolescents will have viewed tens of thousands of commercials portraying the social use of alcohol. They will have seen the use of alcohol glamorized and associated with the most desired things in life: youth, fitness, excitement, entertainment, intimacy, fame, good looks, you name it.

Yet it seems that the media's portrayal of normal behavior, or of social drinking, doesn't ring true for the 13.8 million Americans who meet the criteria for alcohol abuse or alcohol dependence in a given year. This group struggles to consistently moderate their drinking. Alcoholics have long played games with the term consistent when it comes to moderation, and they have failed. The irony of alcoholics attempting to be what they are not is captured in *Alcoholics Anonymous*, the basic text of AA: "The idea that somehow, someday he will control and enjoy his drinking is the obsession of every abnormal drinker."

WHY HIT BOTTOM?

There are some who say that therapy that teaches moderate drinking may help alcoholics in denial conclude that they cannot drink socially. But this is akin to letting someone hit bottom for no good reason. Imagine telling your patient or a family member of a loved one to go ahead and "try moderate drinking and if you wreak havoc on your family, lose your job, threaten your own life as well as that of others behind the wheel, then you should probably try an abstinence-based model of treatment."

The issue of controlled drinking versus abstinence really strikes to the definition of addiction, and unfortunately there is no "blood test" that positively identifies or predicts when a person will cross that fine line between problem drinking and alcoholism. Sometimes it is obvious. Oftentimes, only a comprehensive assessment can differentiate between problem drinking and alcoholism. We can say that heavy drinking episodes may be symptomatic of the early stage of alcoholism or that they are symptomatic of other life issues that need to be resolved—or they will put the person at risk for alcoholism.

WHAT RESEARCH SAYS ABOUT CONTROLLED DRINKING

I expect the issue of teaching moderate drinking will continue to surface. Over the years there have been research reports showing that some alcoholics have returned to controlled drinking. However, they are controversial. In a review of studies of controlled drinking in The Natural History of Alcoholism Revisited, author George Vaillant summed up his findings: "The conclusion, then, should not be that alcohol-dependent individuals never return to social drinking but only that it is a rare and often an unstable state."

Vaillant cited a 1987 longitudinal study by Nordstrom and Berglund that found that of the best outcomes from 324 alcoholics, only 15 returned to controlled drinking for five or more years. He also cited a 1985 outcome survey by Helzer and colleagues, considered one of the most reliable studies, that found that only 2 percent of alcoholics returned to social drinking for more than one or two years.

In 1976 the Rand Corporation published an 18-month follow-up study of 922 alcoholics for the National Institute on Alcohol Abuse and Alcoholism. The study received national acclaim when it reported promising results for "normal" drinking. "Alcoholics can drink socially" said the headlines splashed across newspapers nationwide, even though the study warned against such conclusions. A few years later, when a four-year follow-up of the same alcoholic sample was conducted, the outcomes were sobering to say the least. Almost half of the formerly "nonproblem drinkers" had relapsed into "problem drinking." Their health deteriorated and some died. This time the study's authors highlighted the caveat emptor: The authors caution, as they did in their 18-month study, that their report "does not recommend that any alcoholic resume drinking."

Countless people in recovery, including myself and thousands who have been through Hazelden, are glad they didn't heed the headlines.

II

Can alcoholics be conditioned to drink socially? Under such titles as "harm reduction" and "moderation management" that old question has been resurrected. Moderate drinking is certainly a more appealing goal to many problem drinkers than total abstinence. But medical professionals and addictions counselors are unanimous in their opposition. Are they just rigid prohibitionists?

As a lifetime member of the board of directors of the National Council on Alcoholism and Drug Dependence, I must point out that the big problem is that alcoholism is a progressive disease, often labeled as "problem drinking" in its early stages. Monday's cold is the flu on Wednesday and pneumonia on Friday. Most alcoholics are sure they can control their drinking on the next occasion. The result is killing alcoholics, who can expect a normal lifespan if they remain abstinent. For decades I have defined an alcoholic as one who says, "I can quit anytime I want to." Self-deception is so typical of alcoholics that the American Society of Addiction Medicine included the term "denial" in its latest definition. Talk of harm reduction just feeds the denial.

Most research fails to adequately separate true alcoholics from problem drinkers, which makes reports of success misleading. We can't know how many of the latter may progress into true alcoholism. The most thorough research, conducted by Helzer and Associates in 1985, studied five- and seven-year outcomes on 1,289 diagnosed and treated alcoholics, and found only 1.6 percent were successful moderate drinkers. Of that fraction most were female and none showed clear symptoms of true alcoholism. In any case, it would be unethical to suggest to any patient a goal with a failure rate of 98.4 percent.

WHY ALCOHOLICS CANNOT DRINK IN MODERATION

We psychologists know that conditioning is limited in its ability to produce behavioral changes. To attempt to condition alcoholics to drink socially is asking of behavior modification more than it can do. Some have thought one value of controlled-drinking experiments could be that the patient learns for himself what he has not been able to accept from others, that he cannot drink in moderation. Giving all that extra scientific help might destroy the rationalizations of the alcoholic who still thinks he can drink socially "if I really tried." Actually, most uses of conditioning in the field have been to create an aversion against drinking, to condition alcoholics to live comfortably in a drinking society and to learn how to resist pressure to drink. In that we have been reasonably successful, since this is in accord with the physiology and psychology of addiction.

A STRANGE AND SINISTER TREATMENT

The idea that people who are having problems with alcohol should drink a little plays right into the natural denial mechanism which is a symptom of alcoholism. Almost everyone who comes for help with a drinking problem does so only after having major problems in his or her life. To recommend that they use a little of the poison that is destroying them is a strange and sinister treatment for a recognized disease.

Paul Wood, quoted in *Newsday*, July 21, 1995.

The discussion about turning recovered alcoholics into social drinkers started in 1962, but no scientific research had been attempted until 1970, when Mark and Linda Sobell, two psychologists at Patton State Hospital in California with no clinical experience in treating alcoholics, attempted to modify the drinking of chronic alcoholics, not as a treatment goal but just to see whether it could be done. The research literature is largely a record of failure, indicating that the only realistic goal in treatment is total abstinence.

A RECORD OF FAILURE FOR CONTROLLED DRINKING

The prestigious British alcoholism authority Griffith Edwards concluded that research disproved rather than confirmed the Sobell position. Drs. Ruth Fox, Harry Tiebout, Marvin Block and M.M. Glatt were among the authorities who responded in a special reprint from the 1963 *Quarterly Journal of Studies on Alcohol* to the effect that never in the thousands of cases they had treated was there ever a clear instance of a true alcoholic who returned to drinking in moderation. Ewing was determined to prove it could be done by using every technique known to behavior modification, but he also did careful and lengthy follow up—and at the end of four years every one of Ewing's subjects had gotten drunk and he called off the experiment. Finally, Pendery and Maltzman exposed the failure of the Sobell work, using hospital and police records and direct contact to show that 19 of their 20 subjects did not maintain sobriety in social drinking, and the other probably was not a true alcoholic to begin with.

The research of Peter Nathan indicates that whereas others

may be able to use internal cues (subjective feelings of intoxication) to estimate blood-alcohol level while drinking, alcoholics cannot; so that method of control is not available to them. To ask a recovered addict to engage in "responsible heroin shooting" or a compulsive gambler to play just for small amounts is to ignore the whole psychology and physiology of addiction. Alcoholism is not a simple learned behavior that can be unlearned, but a habitual disposition that has profoundly modified the whole person, mind and body. That explains the admitted failure of psychoanalysis to achieve any notable success in treating alcoholics, and renders vapid the notion of Claude Steiner in "Games Alcoholics Play" that the alcoholic is a naughty child rather than a sick adult. Even the Sobells' claimed successful cases are now reported to have given up controlled drinking. For them abstinence is easier—for them trying to take one drink and stop is sheer misery. The reason is that one cannot "unlearn" the instant euphoric reinforcement that alcohol gives.

"Among heroin addicts receiving
[methadone], heroin use typically
drops 69 percent, cocaine use by 48
percent and crime by 52 percent."

METHADONE IS AN EFFECTIVE TREATMENT FOR HEROIN ADDICTION

Stephen Chapman

In methadone treatment programs, heroin addicts are given the opiate drug methadone to stave off withdrawal symptoms and reduce the cravings for heroin. Nationally syndicated columnist Stephen Chapman maintains in the following viewpoint that methadone is the most effective way to treat heroin addicts. He asserts that methadone treatment programs reduce drug use and drug-related problems such as crime and the spread of disease through shared needles.

As you read, consider the following questions:

1. According to Chapman, what are some of the positive results of methadone treatment?
2. What barriers to methadone treatment do addicts currently face, in the author's view?
3. As cited by Chapman, what support for methadone is offered by drug czar Barry McCaffrey?

Reprinted from Stephen Chapman, "Saving Us from a Cure for Drug Abuse," *Conservative Chronicle*, October 14, 1998, by permission of Stephen Chapman and Creators Syndicate.

Anyone with a broken ankle is grateful for the invention of crutches, and anyone who loathes mice is likely to look favorably upon mousetraps. Those suffering from a problem normally welcome a solution. But heroin addiction is different. In this country, government bodies that claim to want to stamp out this scourge actually seem more determined to get rid of the cure.

Physicians know how to treat heroin addiction: with a medicine called methadone, which, when administered once a day, satisfies the user's cravings while allowing him to function normally. A 1990 report by the Institute of Medicine at the National Academy of Sciences found that of all the drug treatments known to man, "methadone maintenance has been the most rigorously studied and has yielded the most incontrovertibly positive results.

What sort of positive results? Just stuff like reducing drug use, crime and disease among addicts, while boosting their ability to hold jobs and stay off welfare. Methadone, says Mark Kleiman, a professor of public policy at UCLA, "is a real magic bullet." It can be safely used for decades.

BARRIERS TO METHADONE TREATMENT

But the only people treated with more suspicion than people who use heroin are people who want to help them stop using heroin. Methadone is supervised like the gold in Fort Knox, subject to rules stricter than those for any other pharmaceutical drug.

Addicts can't get it from their doctors—they have to go to special clinics, which are burdened with an array of regulations on staffing, security and so on. And since these special clinics attract—surprise!—heroin addicts, not many neighborhoods greet them with brass bands. New York Mayor Rudy Giuliani wants to get the city entirely out of the business of dispensing methadone, insisting that users should be able to abstain from heroin without relying on another drug.

Given the resistance, methadone clinics are scarce, and they tend to be in seedy urban areas far away from, and uninviting to, many middle-class users. The main achievement of these policies is to prevent addicts from getting help. For each one in treatment, experts say, there are another two or three who would get it if they could.

Hard-line drug warriors generally have no use for methadone. They complain that it merely substitutes one opiate for another—which is true and which is like saying that nicotine patches are as bad as cigarettes. Yes, methadone is a drug that many patients have to take for the rest of their lives to stay clean. But plenty of people take medications every day to alleviate ailments, from insulin to Prozac, without being verbally abused by Rudy Giuliani. Some heroin users can kick the habit without methadone. But that's no reason to abandon the ones who can't.

THE NEED FOR MORE METHADONE TREATMENT

Even drug czar Barry McCaffrey, whose views do not always converge with my own, sees the wisdom of expanding methadone treatment. Not long ago, the White House drug czar was making disparaging claims about the effects of the Netherlands' tolerance of marijuana use, and I was suggesting that he wouldn't know how to pour water out of a boot if the instructions were written on the heel. But McCaffrey is not always impervious to evidence. Recently, he journeyed to Mayor Giuliani's fiefdom to argue that what we need is not less methadone treatment but more.

A PRACTICAL AND EFFECTIVE CURE

When the first patients were given up to 80 milligrams of methadone once a day in double-blind studies lasting eight weeks, Dr. Mary Jeanne Kreek, head of the Laboratory of the Biology of Addictive Diseases at Rockefeller University, said, "they began turning away from drug administration and getting on with their lives." The researchers found that a dose of 80 milligrams of methadone, costing less than a dollar, could block the effect of $200 worth of heroin bought on the street.

Methadone is practical and effective, Dr. Kreek said, because it can be taken by mouth, its effects are felt gradually and it wears off slowly. Half of it remains in the body after 24 hours. In contrast, heroin's euphoric rush lasts only minutes.

Minor side effects of methadone, including sweating, constipation and a reduced sex drive, tend to disappear when patients adjust to the medication. Dr. Kreek, who has been studying methadone use for 33 years, reported, "There's no deleterious effect, physiologically or in terms of any medical condition, with the use of methadone."

Christopher Wren, *New York Times*, June 3, 1997.

He made an incontestable case, noting studies which find that among heroin addicts receiving this medicine, good things happen. Heroin use typically drops 69 percent, cocaine use by 48 percent and crime by 52 percent—while full-time work rises by 24 percent. People who stop using heroin are also less likely to get AIDS, hepatitis and other nasty diseases. Treatment costs just $13 a day, and the government is likely to save far more than that for every addict it weans off heroin.

For government officials to rail against methadone is like a thirsty man rejecting water—irrational, self-destructive and indicative that the brain has shut down under stress. McCaffrey is trying to bring them to their senses by arguing that heroin addiction should be viewed less as a sin to be punished and more as a disease to be treated—preferably with the best means available.

Giuliani rejects such advice, contending that when it comes to drug abuse, McCaffrey has "surrendered." The mayor, of course, is right. The drug czar has surrendered to facts and reason—unlike Giuliani, who is still fighting them.

What is clearly needed, as McCaffrey suggested, is for laws to stop getting in the way of patients who need a safe and effective drug and doctors who want to prescribe it for them. If addicts could get their medication from ordinary physicians and ordinary pharmacies, they would be more likely to go into treatment and more likely to succeed at it.

> "Reliable junkies with full-time jobs, paying for their own methadone, are few and far between. Most . . . spend their days robbing, stealing, dealing, prostituting themselves, conning relatives and abandoning their kids."

METHADONE IS NOT AN EFFECTIVE TREATMENT FOR HEROIN ADDICTION

Barbara Del Pizzo

Methadone, an opiate drug administered to addicts in order to eliminate their cravings for heroin, has been lauded by many as an effective way to keep addicts clean. However, in the following viewpoint, Barbara Del Pizzo challenges the idea that methadone treatment programs help addicts kick their drug habit. Instead, she claims, most addicts in methadone programs continue to use heroin. Del Pizzo is a writer based in Nyack, New York, and a former heroin addict.

As you read, consider the following questions:

1. According to Del Pizzo, why did methadone use make her recovery more difficult?
2. In the author's view, how do most heroin addicts support themselves?
3. What keeps junkies from getting sober, in Del Pizzo's opinion?

New York Mayor Rudolph Giuliani stirred a furor when he called for the abolition of methadone treatment for heroin addicts in the city—a position that put him at odds with the Clinton administration's drug czar, Gen. Barry McCaffrey. As a recovering addict, I can say that Mr. Giuliani is right: Promising addicts free methadone for life is not doing them a favor.

I am in my 15th year of recovery, following a 26-year habit. Since 1984 I have not used heroin, methadone, codeine, speed, marijuana, cocaine, barbiturates, hypnotics, psychedelics or alcohol.

Like all addicts, I could never get enough: Some days I took half a dozen drugs in combination, seeking the perfect balance between stimulation and relaxation. I ingested them by any means available—drinks, pills, pipes, powders or needles. When I managed to go to work (a series of short-term jobs), I imagined myself a competent employee. I thought no one knew I was high and shooting up in the bathroom. Later I was to learn that my flaky behavior did not go unnoticed.

A NEED FOR LARGER DOSES

Over time, I experienced a gradual increase in tolerance and required progressively larger doses to maintain a basic level of comfort. A shot of heroin or a bottle of methadone keeps withdrawal symptoms at bay for 24 hours—they're interchangeable. But addicts want more than just to feel normal. They want to get high

So after drinking my free dose at the methadone clinic, I would buy extra bottles from the junkies who hung around outside and sold their take-home doses. (These junkies also sold the free needles the clinic gave them in order to buy more drugs; so much for that nostrum.) I squirreled the doses away for later use as a cushion from the brutal, inevitable depression that loomed fatally and irrevocably when the high from other drugs finally ran out.

And other drugs there were. If I missed methadone clinic hours for the day, I could always substitute heroin or any of the synthetic opiates. The longer I stayed on the methadone program, the bigger my habit became. Indeed, methadone use made recovery more difficult, as it provided a consistent base upon which to build my tolerance, something low-quality street drugs didn't always do. Methadone also made my regular drug habit more expensive, as my increased tolerance meant I needed an unusually large fix on the days I missed going to the clinic.

The idea that we want active junkies to be "functioning" members of society is not only bizarre but dangerous. Junkies are by definition self-destructive. Would you want an addict driving the bus your children take to school, or performing heart surgery on your father?

A TROUBLESOME CURE

Most addicts who want to kick heroin are sent to clinics that administer methadone. But that cure is nearly as troublesome as the disease it treats. Methadone produces its own high and is so addictive that it has its own black market. To receive it legally, addicts must report every day to authorized clinics, something many are loath to do. [One user] tried methadone and found the experience a lot like taking heroin—only he had to get his fix in front of a mangy group of drug pushers and criminals. The scene made him feel closer to drugs, not free of them.

John Cloud, *Time*, January 19, 1998.

Luckily, most junkies are too preoccupied to bother with jobs. Many receive the city or county welfare package, which includes subsidized housing, Medicaid and food stamps, or federal welfare known as Supplemental Security Income, which actually pays addicts in cash for their "disability." But should responsible, hard-working taxpayers pay for the drugs, entertainment and living expenses of people who do nothing but get high all day? Reliable junkies with full-time jobs, paying for their own methadone, are few and far between. Most of the ones I know spend their days robbing, stealing, dealing, prostituting themselves, conning relatives and abandoning their kids.

HOW JUNKIES GET SOBER

When the procurement of the drug becomes too difficult, and the high is no longer worth the effort, junkies get sober—unless they manage to find an enabler who will help them procure and pay for their drugs. The hand-wringing lament that "we have no choice, we simply have to supply addicts with drugs to appease them, to keep them from going on a rampage, threatening our neighborhoods, stealing, looting, raping, killing" is absurd. By supplying addicts with drugs or money for drugs, we are not helping them get better. We are abetting their self-destruction.

Weaning addicts off methadone as quickly as possible is the most effective way to correct their dysfunctional lives. They can't be helped so long as they are looking ahead to their next high. Better to let them experience the consequences of their lifestyle so they can hit bottom, surrender and get help.

> "Heroin ... causes very few, if any,
> problems when it is used in a
> controlled fashion and administered
> in hygienic conditions."

HEROIN ADDICTS SHOULD HAVE SUPERVISED ACCESS TO HEROIN

Ethan Nadelmann

Ethan Nadelmann, director of The Lindesmith Center, a drug-policy research institute, argues in favor of prescribing heroin to addicts under supervised conditions. According to Nadelmann, this unique approach to heroin addiction would benefit addicts and society. A Swiss program that supplies addicts with legal heroin has reduced drug-related crime and improved the health of addicts.

As you read, consider the following questions:

1. According to Nadelmann, how is heroin administered in the Swiss heroin-prescription programs?
2. What have the preliminary findings about the Swiss experiment revealed about heroin maintenance, as cited by Nadelmann?
3. In the author's view, why is heroin maintenance a sensible and humane approach to heroin addiction?

Reprinted from Ethan Nadelmann, "Switzerland's Heroin Experiment," *National Review*, July 10, 1995, with permission; ©1995 by National Review, Inc., 215 Lexington Ave., New York, NY 10016.

The Swiss government is selling heroin to hard-core drug users. But in doing so the government isn't offhandedly facilitating drug abuse; it's conducting a national scientific experiment to determine whether prescribing heroin, morphine, and injectable methadone will save Switzerland both money and misery by reducing crime, disease, and death.

The Swiss deal with drug users much as the U.S. and other countries do—prisons, drug-free residential treatment programs, oral methadone, etc.—but they also know that these approaches are not enough. They first tried establishing a "Needle Park" in Zurich, an open drug scene where people could use drugs without being arrested. Most Zurichers, including the police, initially regarded the congregation of illicit drug injectors in one place as preferable to scattering them throughout the city. But the scene grew unmanageable, and city officials closed it down in February 1992. A second attempt faced similar problems and was shut down in March 1995.

How Heroin Prescription Works

So Needle Park wasn't the solution, but the heroin-prescription program might be. In it, 340 addicts receive a legal supply of heroin each day from one of the nine prescribing programs in eight different cities. In addition, 11 receive morphine, and 33 receive injectable methadone. The programs accept only "hard-core" junkies—people who have been injecting for years and who have attempted and failed to quit. Participants are not allowed to take the drug home with them. They have to inject on site and pay 15 francs (approximately $13) per day for their dose.

The idea of prescribing heroin to junkies in hopes of reducing both their criminal activity and their risk of spreading AIDS and other diseases took off in 1991. Expert scientific and ethical advisory bodies were established to consider the range of issues. The International Narcotics Control Board—a United Nations organization that oversees international antidrug treaties—had to be convinced that the Swiss innovation was an experiment, which is permitted under the treaty, rather than an official shift in policy. In Basel, opponents of the initiative demanded a citywide referendum—in which 65 per cent of the electorate approved a local heroin-prescription program. The argument that swayed most people was remarkably straightforward: only a controlled scientific experiment could determine whether prescribing heroin to addicts is feasible and beneficial.

The experiment started in January 1994. The various programs differ in some respects, although most provide supplemental doses of oral methadone, psychological counseling, and other assistance. Some are located in cities like Zurich, others in towns like Thun, which sits at the foot of the Bernese Alps. Some provide just one drug, while others offer a choice. Some allow clients to vary their dose each day, while others work with clients to establish a stable dosage level. One of the programs in Zurich is primarily for women. The other Zurich program permits addicts to take home heroin-injected cigarettes known as reefers, or "sugarettes," (since heroin is called "sugar" by Swiss junkies). It also conducted a parallel experiment in which 12 clients were prescribed cocaine reefers for up to 12 weeks. The results were mixed, with many of the participants finding the reefers unsatisfying. However, since more than two-thirds of Swiss junkies use cocaine as well as heroin, the Swiss hope to refine the cocaine experiment in the future.

ANSWERING QUESTIONS ABOUT DRUG POLICY

The national experiment is designed to answer a host of questions that also bubble up in debates over drug policy in the United States, but that our drug-war blinders force us to ignore. Can junkies stabilize their drug use if they are assured of a legal, safe, and stable source of heroin? Can they hold down a job even if they're injecting heroin two or three times a day? Do they stop using illegal heroin and cut back on use of other illegal drugs? Do they commit fewer crimes? Are they healthier and less likely to contract the HIV virus? Are they less likely to overdose? Is it possible to overcome the "not in my back yard" objections that so often block methadone and other programs for addicts?

The answers to these questions are just beginning to come in. In late 1994, the Social Welfare Department in Zurich held a press conference to issue its preliminary findings: 1) Heroin prescription is feasible, and has produced no black market in diverted heroin. 2) The health of the addicts in the program has clearly improved. 3) Heroin prescription alone cannot solve the problems that led to the heroin addiction in the first place. 4) Heroin prescription is less a medical program than a social-psychological approach to a complex personal and social problem. 5) Heroin per se causes very few, if any, problems when it is used in a controlled fashion and administered in hygienic conditions.

Program administrators also found little support for the widespread belief that addicts' cravings for heroin are insatiable. When offered practically unlimited amounts of heroin (up to 300 milligrams three times a day), addicts soon realized that the maximum doses provided less of a "flash" than lower doses, and cut back their dosage levels accordingly.

On the basis of these initial findings, the Swiss federal government approved an expansion of the experiment—one that may offer an opportunity to address the bigger question that small-scale experiments and pilot projects cannot answer: Can the controlled prescription of heroin to addicts take the steam out of the illegal drug markets?

A HARM REDUCTION APPROACH

Switzerland's prescription experiment fits in with the two-track strategy Switzerland and other Western European countries have been pursuing since the mid-1980s: tough police measures against drug dealers, and a "harm reduction" approach toward users. The idea behind harm reduction is to stop pretending that a drug-free society is a realistic goal; focus first on curtailing the spread of AIDS—a disease that will have cost the U.S. $15.2 billion by the end of 1995, and the lives of over 125,000 Americans—and later on curtailing drug use.

STABILIZING ADDICTS

Contrary to the public charges that heroin maintenance is "legalized drugs" and only "serves to keep addicts addicted," heroin maintenance programs were tightly controlled clinically supervised protocols with the goal of stabilizing patients to assist them in controlling their addiction and leading toward abstinence. . . .

The Swiss study of heroin maintenance enrolled 1,000 participants. Using American-developed measures, the Swiss investigators reported substantial declines in crime and illegal income. The amount of heroin used (dosing) first leveled off and then started to decline within nine months. Retention rates exceeded those typically reported for treatment. The program had intense supervision and participants made up to three visits per day.

David Vlahov, *Washington Times*, August 16, 1998.

The effort to make sterile syringes more available through needle-exchange programs and the sale of needles in pharmacies and vending machines epitomizes the harm-reduction philosophy. Swiss physicians and pharmacists—along with their professional associations—are outspoken in their support of these initiatives. Study after study, including one conducted for the U.S. Centers for Disease Control, show that increasing needle availability reduces the spread of AIDS, gets dirty syringes off the streets, and saves money.

The Swiss have also created legal Fixerräume, or "injection rooms," where addicts can shoot up in a regulated, sanitary environment. Swiss public-health officials regard this harm-reduction innovation as preferable to the two most likely alternatives: open injection of illicit drugs in public places, which is distasteful and unsettling to most non-addicts; and the more discreet use of drugs in unsanctioned "shooting galleries" that are frequently dirty, violent, controlled by drug dealers, and conducive to needle sharing. Five Fixerräume are now open in Switzerland. Initial evaluations indicate that they are effective in reducing HIV transmission and the risk of overdose.

So what does the future hold? In June 1995, Switzerland's governing body, the Federal Council, voted to expand the number of prescription slots to 1,000: 800 for heroin, 100 each for morphine and injectable methadone. Interior minister Ruth Dreifuss, who initially was skeptical of the experiment, is now a strong supporter. She is backed by the ministers of justice, defense, and finance, who together constitute what has become known as "the drug delegation" of the Federal Council. The three leading political parties have combined to issue a joint report on drug policy that supports the heroin experiment and other harm-reduction initiatives. Outside Switzerland, the Dutch are about to embark on their own modest experiment with heroin prescription. The Australians, who recently conducted an extensive feasibility study, seem likely to start a heroin-prescription program. In Germany, officials in Frankfurt, Hamburg, Karlsruhe, Stuttgart, and elsewhere are seeking permission from the central government to begin their own heroin-prescription projects.

THE U.S. WAR AGAINST DRUG USERS

While these countries experiment with more sensible and humane approaches to drug policy, the United States clings to a war not only against drug dealers, but also against drug users. Most scientific researchers studying drug abuse acknowledge that the Swiss experiment makes sense socially, economically, and morally. The point of these innovations isn't to coddle drug users. It's to reduce the human and economic costs of drug use—costs paid not only by users but also by non-users through increased health-care, justice, and law-enforcement expenditures.

But no distinguished researcher seems prepared to take on all the forces blocking a heroin-prescription experiment in the United States. Through our reticence, we are shutting our eyes to drug policy options that could reduce crime, death, and disease and ultimately save this country billions of dollars.

> "[Proponents of heroin maintenance] want to keep judgment-impaired addicts in their deadly lifestyle until they die or quit by chance."

SUPPLYING ADDICTS WITH HEROIN IS DANGEROUS

Robert Maginnis

Robert Maginnis contends in the following viewpoint that programs to supply addicts with heroin will encourage drug legalization, increase drug use, and lead to the death of many addicts. According to Maginnis, studies documenting the success of the Swiss heroin maintenance experiment are flawed. Maginnis is a senior policy adviser with the Family Research Council, a nonprofit educational organization promoting the traditional family unit and the Judeo-Christian value system.

As you read, consider the following questions:

1. How was the Swiss heroin maintenance program scientifically flawed, in the author's view?
2. What evidence of the Swiss experiment's failure does Maginnis provide?
3. In Maginnis's opinion, why is it unethical to give heroin to addicts?

Reprinted from Robert Maginnis, "Treat Addicts with Drug Maintenance? Disputed Results," *The Washington Times*, August 16, 1998, by permission of the author.

European drug legalizers have long touted the merits of heroin giveaways. Now, those same people want to give heroin to addicts in Baltimore—where almost half of all adults arrested test positive for opiates. If Baltimore's "pilot" program is declared a "success," expect heroin giveaways to spread across America.

Heroin giveaways are an extension of the "harm reduction" philosophy that says drug use cannot be eliminated, so society should try to "reduce the harm" it causes. The best known "harm reduction" programs are needle exchanges. Both programs pave the way for drug legalization, increased drug use, and the certain deaths of many addicts.

The Baltimore Sun quoted that city's health commissioner, Dr. Peter Beilenson, who said, "It will be politically difficult but I think it's going to happen. He claims heroin "maintenance"—a euphemism for giving pharmaceutical-grade heroin to addicts in an effort to improve their physical and social well-being—"would be carefully controlled by health care providers."

PROMOTING HEROIN FOR "MEDICAL" REASONS

Dr. Beilenson's announcement comes on the heels of a June 6, 1998, New York City seminar promoting heroin for "medical" reasons. Billionaire George Soros, the nation's leading drug legalizer, was the primary event sponsor. A seminar attendee David Vlahov, a professor at the Johns Hopkins School of Public Health in Baltimore, is involved in planning the nation's first heroin program.

Messrs. Vlahov and Beilenson have Baltimore Mayor Kurt Schmoke's full support. Mr. Schmoke is a board member of the pro-legalization, Soros-sponsored Drug Policy Foundation. In May 1997, Mr. Schmoke urged President Clinton at the National Mayors Conference to endorse heroin maintenance.

At the New York heroin seminar, Messrs. Vlahov and Beilenson were impressed by Switzerland's recent three-year study. Mr. Vlahov said "heroin maintenance is an outreach strategy to bring people into the [treatment] system."

Dr. Beilenson claims a U.S. version of the Swiss program would help most addicts become drug-free and reduce both crime and homelessness. The Swiss heroin experiment began in 1994. The project, which officially ended in December 1996, involved 1,146 addicts who paid nominal fees for up to three injections a day to determine whether giving heroin to addicts could "normalize" their lives.

In July 1997, the Swiss government labeled the experiment a "success."

Some outsiders disagree with this assessment. The World Health Organization labeled the heroin trials as "quasi-experimental" and Dr. Oskar Schroeder, the then-president of the United Nations International Narcotics Control Board, called Switzerland's heroin experiment "a first step toward legalization."

A FLAWED EXPERIMENT

The Swiss project was scientifically flawed. Neither the number of addicts nor the mix of participants receiving heroin, morphine or methadone was held constant. The initial goal of abstinence was abandoned in favor of a "better understanding of heroin addiction." Prison inmates and mental patients were added midway through the project. Most of the new heroin "patients" (61 percent) were taken from methadone programs (a synthetic opiate that blocks the effects of heroin), and 19 percent weren't even heroin addicts before the Swiss government started drug dealing.

WHY HEROIN MAINTENANCE CANNOT WORK

Nobody ever kicked a heroin or cocaine habit while simultaneously injecting drugs. Tapering off with some kind of Nicotrol patch is a delusion with which every drug addict lives. Such an idea is absurd.

Michael Balfe Howard, *Rocky Mountain News*, October 30, 1997.

Thomas Zeltner, director of the Swiss Federal Office of Public Health, participated in the New York heroin conference. He said heroin maintenance is part of a "holistic approach" to solving the drug problem.

Mr. Zeltner does not believe a drug-free society is possible, but admits heroin projects are not a panacea and "may not work for other nations." It's not clear heroin giveaways work for Switzerland. More Swiss addicts died while in the program than became drug-free. As for crime rates, police were not included in the experiment's design and operation, so reported crime decreases were exclusively based on self-reporting by addicts rather than law enforcement data.

Addicts' health improved not because they were given free dope, but because they were provided routine health care, food and housing. Addicts' employment did rise for menial public service jobs, but so did welfare dependency.

Baltimore's Dr. Beilenson was joined at the heroin conference by health researchers and officials from cities like Chicago, New

Haven, San Antonio, and Sacramento. These officials are rightly concerned about the growing heroin scourge. Unfortunately, they embrace the Swiss model and are planning an American heroin pilot program run by universities with private funds. Any trial must first be approved by federal oversight agencies, however.

An Unethical Approach

Giving heroin to addicts is unethical and can result in euthanasia. Instead of embracing the tough-love drug court approach of coercing addicts into life-saving treatment, "harm reductionists" want to keep judgment-impaired addicts in their deadly lifestyle until they die or quit by chance.

America should focus anti-drug efforts on a balanced model of enforcement, abstinence-based treatment and prevention.

> "Holistic therapies . . . take away
> some of the underlying causes of
> [substance] abuse by helping people
> become aware of and take
> responsibility for the way they
> think, feel, and act."

HOLISTIC THERAPIES CAN HELP ADDICTS RECOVER

Marianne Apostolides

Marianne Apostolides describes in the following viewpoint how holistic therapies benefit people suffering from addiction. Apostolides, who writes for Psychology Today, claims that therapies such as massage, yoga, nutritional therapy, acupuncture, hypnosis, and homeopathy lessen the impact of withdrawal symptoms and prevent addicts from relapsing.

As you read, consider the following questions:

1. How does holistic philosophy overlap with the harm-reduction approach to addiction, in the author's view?
2. According to Apostolides, how does massage benefit people recovering from an addiction?
3. How is acupuncture used to treat addiction?

Abridged from Marianne Apostolides, "How to Quit the Holistic Way," Psychology Today, September/October 1996. Reprinted with permission from Psychology Today magazine. Copyright ©1996 (Sussex Publishers, Inc.).

They've been minimized and they've been marginalized, but the fact is holistic therapies—including acupuncture, homeopathy, massage therapy, aromatherapy, yoga, nutrition therapy, and dozens more—have been gaining greater mainstream acceptance. According to a 1993 survey published in the *New England Journal of Medicine*, in 1991, about 21 million Americans made 425 million visits to practitioners of these types of alternative medicine; that's more than the estimated 388 million visits we made to all primary care physicians that year. Now a holistic approach—where an individual's situation and particular way of coping is addressed, and going cold turkey may not be necessary—is slowly beginning to influence the way people with addictions are treated. Holistic therapies are helping to bridge the gap between conventional, exclusively abstinence-oriented approaches and the newer, more controversial harm-reduction philosophy.

When addressing an addiction, all holistic techniques begin with the same basic philosophy: people develop addictions to correct an "imbalance" within them. Addicts become stuck, unaware, and unable to deal with their thoughts, feelings, and actions. They may drink, take drugs, or eat to excess to disassociate from their deficiency. Holistic therapies work to restore balance by connecting mind and body. They take away some of the underlying causes of abuse by helping people become aware of and take responsibility for the way they think, feel, and act.

The goal of many holistic therapies is to restore the body to its naturally healthy state. The best treatments are not offered in isolation; they're carried out with psychotherapy or group therapy—especially when it's open to the holistic view of treating the entire person, not just the addiction—and other holistic therapies.

HOLISTIC PHILOSOPHY AND HARM REDUCTION

Holistic philosophy overlaps with the harm-reduction approach to addiction, which evolved out of a desire to slow the spread of HIV/AIDS and hepatitis among injection drug users by dispensing clean needles. People running syringe exchanges realized they had an opportunity to provide additional services to drug users. Now a number of harm-reduction centers—offering programs including acupuncture, massage therapy, and substance use counseling; referrals to detoxification and treatment facilities; and caseworkers to help with housing, food stamps, and medical care—have sprung up in cities like New York, Chicago, Portland, Seattle, Los Angeles, Santa Cruz, San Francisco, and

Oakland. Run by current and former drug users, for current and former drug users, these centers don't demand that clients remain abstinent. From experience they know that no one can be forced into dealing with a problem, and that people who are treated with respect and who are educated about their choices can and often do elect to help themselves.

Holistic therapies do have their skeptics, of course. There's concern that these therapies haven't been properly studied or regulated. "As a general rule, holistic therapies are most helpful when they're used in conjunction with—not in place of—other treatments, says Barrie R. Cassileth, Ph.D., an adjunct professor of medicine at the University of North Carolina at Chapel Hill and Duke University, who has written extensively on alternative therapies and cancer treatment. Cassileth sees the need for methodologically sound, rigorous clinical tests before any claims about the capabilities of holistic treatments can be made. Frank Gawin, M.D., scientific director of a laboratory examining addictions at the University of California at Los Angeles, agrees. He's currently involved in a six-city study—the largest involving an alternative therapy—to determine the effectiveness of acupuncture on cocaine addiction. Dr. Gawin believes that holistic therapies should continue to be practiced while studies are underway, so long as people receive psychotherapy and are fully informed that these treatments have not been proven effective. "There are no magic bullets," Cassileth concludes. "People ought to be wary of those who say they have one."

MASSAGE

It's too simplistic to say an addiction can be massaged away, but the power of this hands-on therapy is being tested on people dealing with anorexia, bulimia, smoking, and other addictions, with impressive results. The mind-body connection is all-important in massage, says Elliot Greene, M.A., past president of the American Massage Therapy Association. Greene says people with addictions can become trapped in a cycle of avoiding their problems and disassociating from their bodies. The experience of massage—where someone touches, respects, and cares for a person's body—can break that cycle, helping addicts reconnect physically and center themselves emotionally. The effect is a newly empowered person more able to talk about and come to terms with an addiction.

Massage may also have a powerful chemical impact on the body. By massaging the soft tissue, therapists release tension and get energy moving. The loosening of tight muscles sends the body a signal to cut down production of stress hormones, such as cortisol. This neurological response has a calming effect on body and mind. In addition, massage moves lymph through the body, assisting the body's natural cleansing process.

Various research is now testing the effectiveness of massage therapy. At the Touch Research Institute at the University of Miami Medical School, 48 different studies are currently underway to determine the effectiveness of massage on problems, such as anorexia and bulimia, drug addiction, asthma, and diabetes. In one ongoing study looking at massage's effects on tobacco addiction, smokers were taught to massage their ears and hands when they craved a cigarette. After one month, they had reduced the number of cigarettes smoked—and their cravings for them—by 40 percent. There will be a follow-up at three and six months to see if the results hold. "Massage provides a distraction that takes away from the nervous-habit aspect of smoking," says Tiffany Field, Ph.D., the institute's director.

HATHA YOGA

Hatha yoga, the yoga of postures—where people hold positions for varying lengths of time, stretching and contracting their muscles and breathing deeply—is one component of the ancient practice of yoga. It simulates the relaxing effects of the parasympathetic nervous system and removes tension from all the major muscle groups. According to Joseph LePage, founder and director of Integrative Yoga Therapy in Aptos, California, certain postures actually massage internal organs, helping dispel toxins that may have built up in the liver and kidneys from substance abuse.

"Hatha yoga allows people to get back in touch with themselves, and get into a frame of mind where they can experience what it is to be well, and not drug dependent or anxious," explains Peter Stein, M.A., addictions specialist at the North Charles Institute for the Addictions, a private treatment facility in Boston, Massachusetts. According to a clinical trial by Howard Shaffer, Ph.D., director of the Division on Addictions at Harvard Medical School, hatha yoga is as effective as traditional group therapy in treating heroin addicts enrolled at a Boston methadone maintenance clinic. Those who practiced yoga for 75 minutes once a week and received individual therapy once a week reduced their drug use, criminal activity, and cravings as much as those who went to group therapy once a week and had individual counseling.

Joyce, 37, a manager at a gourmet food store in the Boston area, has combined hatha yoga with talk therapy for four years as a part of her methadone maintenance program. Although methadone has been essential to her getting off heroin, she now wants to give it up. "Yoga helps me become more aware physically, and then become aware mentally of what's going on with me, and of how the things I do affect other people," she says. "Five years ago, I'd have told you I'd be on methadone for the rest of my life. But now I'm in a different frame of mind."

Joyce has begun slowly detoxing off methadone, which is itself a physically addicting drug whose withdrawal symptoms are cold sweats, inability to sleep, impatience, and discomfort. "In yoga, you have to hold postures for so long, and while you're holding them, you're saying to yourself 'I know this hurts, but I know I have to do it, I can and want to do it myself.'" That experience of feeling and withstanding the physical pain in hatha yoga helps Joyce know she can withstand the physical pain of methadone withdrawal.

NUTRITION THERAPY

"When people think of nutrition, I want them to think of the biochemical substances that are essential for maintaining optimal brain chemistry," says nutritionist Joan Mathews-Larson, Ph.D., founder of the Health Recovery Center (HRC), a private abstinence-based addiction clinic in Minneapolis, Minnesota. After people change their diets and supplement their food intake with the right amount of amino acids, essential fatty acids, vitamins, and minerals, they can begin to deal with their alcoholism, drug abuse, anorexia, or bulimia, says Julia Ross, M.A., executive director of Recovery Systems, a private eating-disorder and drug-abuse facility in San Francisco, California.

With the proper nutrition and supplements, the brain manufactures chemicals—like norepinephrine, a neurotransmitter that seems to increase energy and boost mood; serotonin, another important neurotransmitter; and endorphins, the brain's natural opiates—that are needed to regulate mood and behavior.

Optimal nutrition may also correct the possible deficiencies that contribute to alcoholism or substance abuse. "The question," says Alan Gaby, M.D., editor of the Nutrition and Healing newsletter, "is what are the proper supplements? I treated an alcoholic who couldn't control his drinking, but with glutamine, an amino acid, he was able to go back to social drinking and handle it." For cocaine addiction, Dr. Gaby says the amino acid tyrosine is often recommended. Tyrosine is a building block for norepinephrine.

Richard Firshein, D.O., a New York City osteopath whose

holistic practice emphasizes nutritional healing, says one theory is that addiction may be triggered by low levels of serotonin. By restoring healthy levels, one of the underlying causes of addiction can be taken away. Firshein prescribes a combination of amino acids and a high-carbohydrate diet to boost tryptophan, the building block for serotonin.

Vitamin C is sometimes used by nutrition therapists to moderate both the physical and emotional withdrawal symptoms of detoxification. "It was being used for some time with narcotics addicts," says Dr. Gaby. "The most dramatic case I've seen was a patient who sniffed morphine every day. He came to me on his second day of withdrawal. His shakes were so bad that he couldn't sit still. I gave him an intravenous injection of about 4 grams of vitamin C, along with magnesium, calcium, and B vitamins. About halfway through the injection he calmed down, and ultimately his withdrawal symptoms subsided. That lasted about 36 hours. He had to come back for three more injections over five days, but he essentially went through withdrawal without symptoms."

After detoxification, nutrients such as niacin, chromium, and magnesium are given to alleviate hypoglycemic reactions, which a high percentage of alcoholics, as well as a lesser number of amphetamine and heroin users, experience. Hypoglycemia, a metabolic condition that results in low levels of glucose in the brain, can cause depression, anxiety, panic attacks, and mood swings, perhaps bringing about more substance abuse. , , ,

ACUPUNCTURE

Acupuncture's use as a treatment for addiction was discovered in 1972 by Wen, a Hong Kong neurosurgeon. Testing its use as an anesthetic, he accidentally determined—because many of his volunteers were opium addicts—that it reduced withdrawal symptoms such as nausea and the shakes. Since Wen's discovery, acupuncture has become the most widespread holistic therapy for treating addictions to cocaine, alcohol, nicotine, and heroin.

Like much of traditional Chinese medicine, acupuncture works on the theory that networks of energy, called chi, flow through the body along natural pathways, and disease grows when that energy is out of balance or blocked. By inserting needles at precise positions along these pathways, acupuncturists aim to stimulate the body's flow of energy, restoring balance.

For an addiction, most people receive auricular (ear) acupuncture because yin energy—the nurturing energy that's damaged by an addiction—can be manipulated at points on the ear. Typically, an auricular acupuncturist will place five needles in the ear. The points used are: shen-men (the 'spirit gate') an often-used acupuncture point that slows the heart rate and calms anxiety; the sympathetic nervous system point, which relaxes nerves, reduces 'fight or flight' panic, improves digestion, and aids the respiratory system; the kidney point, which helps release toxins through urine and is associated with restoration, rejuvenation, and a deep level of healing and purification of blood; the liver point, which cleanses the body of toxins and is related to emotional balance and stability; and the lung point, a nourishing organ that improves the immune system and eases breathing.

Acupuncturists learn how to touch and relate to their patients, respect their space, and express sympathy. In addition to the biological effects of acupuncture, this kind of care gives patients a sense of confidence, calmness, and motivation to start or continue treatment, says Michael O. Smith, M.D., a psychiatrist and director of Substance Abuse at the Acupuncture Clinic at Lincoln Hospital in New York City, where between 3,000 and 4,000 auricular acupuncturists have been trained.

TREATING ALCOHOLISM WITH ACUPUNCTURE

A 1989 study published in the British journal The Lancet by Milton L. Bullock concluded that acupuncture was highly effective in treating alcoholism. Eighty severe recidivist alcoholics were treated, receiving either correct-point acupuncture or acupuncture at non-specific points on the ear. 21 of the 40 treatment group patients completed the two-month program, while only one of 40 in the control group did. The control group patients experienced twice as many relapses in the six months following the experiment and the number of control group patients admitted to detoxification centers was well over twice that of treatment group patients.

Judd R. Spray and Sharon M. Jones, News Briefs, September 1995.

Acupuncture is used at all stages of an addiction, from the time people seek help to the time they are abstinent. It can ease the discomfort of withdrawal symptoms, including insomnia, muscle ache, profuse sweating, and nausea for heroin; depression, cravings, and fatigue for cocaine; and seizures, diarrhea, and hypertension for alcohol. Additionally, acupuncture may help people stay off drugs after they've gone through withdrawal. By enabling people to clear their minds and decrease stress, anxiety, depression, and cravings, acupuncture can help people deal with the issues that caused their addiction. "It helps people settle down and center themselves so they can participate in their own internal growth," says Dr. Smith. "They're less defensive, more thoughtful, and more open-minded."

From 1991 to 1996, acupuncture's use in addiction has spread to more than 300 clinics. Even the government has given its tacit approval of the therapy: almost half of the drug treatment facilities linked to U.S. drug courts include acupuncture in their programs. Yale University Medical School's Arthur Margolin, Ph.D., who, along with Dr. Gawin, is part of the six-city project looking into the effectiveness of acupuncture on cocaine abuse, says funding for this research came about because there's no pharmacological treatment for cocaine addiction—a vaccine has proven effective in rats—while heroin addicts are often treated with methadone. The problem, says Margolin, is that accurate clinical trials are difficult to design and assess. For example, the placebo in an acupuncture trial requires inserting needles into inactive points, but scientists are not certain which points are truly inactive.

HYPNOSIS

Hypnosis seems helpful in treating addictions, and the depression and anxiety associated with them, according to Michael Yapko, Ph.D., a psychologist with a specialty in hypnosis, and author of Trance Work. Hypnosis aids people with addictions because of its ability to facilitate a heightened state of consciousness. "During hypnosis," Yapko says, "people are intensely focused and their awareness deepened. But even in a trance they can have a conversation."

Not only does hypnosis help people develop specific techniques for changing their addictive behavior, but these techniques seem to take hold more strongly. "Situations, like being in a bar, feel more real than when you're just talking them through in therapy," says Helmut Relinger, Ph.D., a Berkeley, California, psychologist and hypnotherapist. "So people get to rehearse coping with their urges to use," which usually last only one to two minutes. The chance to imagine and truly feel yourself dealing with cravings while hypnotized can help you cope with them at other times.

Brian Alman, Ph.D., a psychologist and creator of Six Steps to Freedom, a program that incorporates self-hypnosis, meditation, and visualization to treat various addictions, says self-hypnosis "allows people to take a unique observer perspective on their own life. They can step back and watch what's going on without judging or criticizing themselves. Alman has begun a two-year study to compare the efficacy of his program with traditional inpatient treatment, AA, and no intervention.

When it comes to nicotine addiction, hypnosis results have been mixed, in part because not everyone can be hypnotized. Its been known for 20 years that people who are easily hypnotized are twice as likely to cut their smoking in half as those who aren't able to go under. Other research indicates the ability of hypnosis to control the pain of drug withdrawal symptoms: Studies on migraines, childbirth and dentistry show that hypnosis allows people to gain control over their fear and anxiety, thereby reducing pain.

HOMEOPATHY

Homeopathy, a 200-year-old system of natural medicine, uses minuscule or extremely diluted amounts of substances that in their original concentration might actually produce symptoms of the disease being treated. This philosophy of "like cures like" doesn't mean a little heroin cures a heroin addiction. In fact, Ed Gogek, M.D., a licensed homeopath, cautions that homeopathy doesn't cure chemical dependencies. But it does work on other problems, like pain, anxiety, depression, and restlessness. In other words, homeopaths don't treat chemical dependencies, they treat the *causes* and *consequences* of addiction, whether to nicotine, cocaine, or food.

A homeopath takes into account a person's mental, emotional, and physical symptoms and uses remedies derived from plant, mineral, and animal sources that best fit a client's particular condition. For drug addiction, these substances may include tuberculinum, argentum, nitricum, arsenicum, or other materials equally unknown to most people. "Substances used in homeopathy help to express and dispel symptoms and regain balance," explains Martha Oelman, media liaison for the National Center for Homeopathy.

The effectiveness of homeopathy is still not clear. So far, the approximately 15 separate studies that have been rigorously re-examined show positive results for conditions like chronic pain, respiratory infections, and trauma.

A 1993 study by Susan Garcia-Swain, M.D., addiction specialist at St. Peter's Chemical Dependency Center in Olympia, Washington, examined 700 people overcoming drug addictions over a three-year period at the Starting Point addiction clinic in San Diego, California. One-third of her patients received counseling and one of 19 homeopathic remedies for addiction withdrawal symptoms; one-third received counseling and a placebo; and the last group received counseling only. The patients who received homeopathic remedies, says Dr. Garcia-Swain, were twice as likely as the others to remain sober after 18 months. Dr. Garcia-Swain says those people treated with homeopathic remedies were better able to benefit from other talk therapies because they were less guarded, more confident, and more inclined to continue in the program.

With a holistic approach to addiction, people with dependencies are given an opportunity to find their own rhythm to recovery. And when you're trying to kick a habit of any sort, that kind of flexibility can be the difference between success and failure.

Periodical Bibliography

The following articles have been selected to supplement the diverse views presented in this chapter. Addresses are provided for periodicals not indexed in the *Readers' Guide to Periodical Literature*, the *Alternative Press Index*, the *Social Sciences Index*, or the *Index to Legal Periodicals and Books*.

Jonathan P. Caulkins — "Yes: Treatment Is More Cost-Effective Than Law Enforcement," *Insight*, June 12, 1995. Available from 3600 New York Ave. NE, Washington, DC 20002.

John Cloud — "A Way Out for Junkies?" *Time*, January 19, 1998.

Geoffrey Cowley — "A New Assault on Addiction," *Newsweek*, January 30, 1995.

Tom Fennell — "Addiction Relief: A Cleansing Therapy Gets People off Heroin," *Maclean's*, December 29, 1997.

Lisa W. Foderaro — "Can Problem Drinkers Really Just Cut Back?" *New York Times*, May 28, 1995.

Audrey Kishline — "A Toast to Moderation," *Psychology Today*, January/February 1996.

Caroline Knapp — "Still One Day at a Time," *New York Times*, August 10, 1998.

Michael J. Lemanski — "The Tenacity of Addiction in the Treatment of Addiction," *Humanist*, May/June 1997.

Anthony Lewis — "The Noble Experiment," *New York Times*, January 5, 1998.

Charles Marwick — "Physician Leadership on National Drug Policy Finds Addiction Treatment Works," *JAMA*, April 15, 1998. Available from the American Medical Association, PO Box 10946, Chicago, IL 60610-0946.

Michael J. Meyers — "Promising Procedure Needs More Study," *Professional Counselor*, October 1997. Available from PO Box 420235, Palm Coast, FL 32142-0235.

David J. Morrow — "Curbing the Urge to Drink: Drug to Treat Alcoholism Sets Off Controversy in U.S.," *New York Times*, July 31, 1998.

Robert E. Solomon — "Sleeping Through Detox," *Professional Counselor*, October 1997.

How Should the Government Deal with Addiction?

CHAPTER PREFACE

In November 1996, Arizona voters approved a ballot initiative that permits illegal drugs to be prescribed for certain illnesses, provided that two doctors agree on the treatment and provide scientific research to back up their approach. The measure also allows drug users the option of probation and drug treatment in lieu of jail for their first two convictions, and prohibits the incarceration of nonviolent drug offenders until their third conviction.

Phoenix surgeon Jeffrey Singer, a spokesperson for the ballot measure, claims that the new law reflects the public's attitudes toward drug abuse and addiction. According to Singer, research conducted on attitudes toward current drug policy showed that people "firmly rejected the policy of 'do drugs, do time.' They believed treatment was much more appropriate than imprisonment for drug users. This belief was so strong that they were willing to parole offenders already in prison. Furthermore, they believed that when it came to prescribing drugs—even marijuana, heroin, and LSD—the patient/doctor relationship should supersede government control."

However, the shift away from a punitive approach to drug use is by no means widespread, especially among government officials, who plan to attack Arizona's law by prosecuting doctors who prescribe illegal substances and removing their licenses. The Clinton administration and drug czar Barry McCaffrey oppose Arizona's approach to drug abuse on the grounds that in a time when marijuana use is increasing among teenagers, relaxing drug laws sends the wrong message about drugs to young people. Furthermore, Maricopa County Attorney Richard Romley says that the initiative is dangerous because it de-emphasizes the dangers of drug use. Protesting the law, Romley pleaded, "I ask America to sit in my chair for a bit and see how many children are abused and how much domestic violence occurs because of people under the influence of drugs."

Although measures such as the Arizona initiative are controversial, most people agree that—as evidenced by the high numbers of drug addicts in jail and on the streets—current drug policy is not working. The proposals for reform range from stricter law enforcement measures to the legalization of all illicit drugs. In the following chapter, authors offer diverse opinions on the proper role of government in dealing with addiction.

"Drug laws harm users of drugs well beyond any harm caused by drug use itself."

LEGALIZING DRUGS WOULD BENEFIT ADDICTS AND SOCIETY

Randy E. Barnett

In the following viewpoint, Randy E. Barnett claims that drug laws cause more harm to addicts and society than drugs themselves. According to Barnett, drug prohibition makes drugs so expensive that addicts turn to crime in order to obtain money to buy them. Furthermore, drug prohibition is unfair in that it punishes users for committing a "crime" that has no victim. Barnett is the author of a number of books about the legal system, including *The Structure of Liberty: Justice and the Rule of the Law*.

As you read, consider the following questions:

1. How do higher prices make drug use more hazardous for users, in Barnett's opinion?
2. According to the author, what harms are unavoidable as long as force is used to minimize drug use?
3. What are two ways that drug laws negatively impact the general public, as stated by Barnett?

Excerpted from Randy E. Barnett, "Curing the Drug-Law Addiction: The Harmful Side Effects of Legal Prohibition," in *Dealing with Drugs: Consequences of Government Control*, edited by Ronald Hamowy (San Francisco: Pacific Research Institute, 1997). Reprinted by permission of the author.

Some drugs make people feel good. That is why some people use them. Some of these drugs are alleged to have side effects so destructive that many advise against their use. The same may be said about statutes that attempt to prohibit the manufacture, sale, and use of drugs. Using statutes in this way makes some people feel good because they think they are "doing something" about what they believe to be a serious social problem. Others who support these laws are not so altruistically motivated. Employees of law enforcement bureaus and academics who receive government grants to study drug use, for example, may gain financially from drug prohibition. But as with using drugs, using drug laws can have moral and practical side effects so destructive that they argue against ever using legal institutions in this manner.

One might even say—and not altogether metaphorically—that some people become psychologically or economically addicted to drug laws. That is, some people continue to support these statutes despite the massive and unavoidable ill effects that result. The psychologically addicted ignore these harms so that they can attain the "good"—their "high"—they perceive that drug laws produce. Other drug-law users ignore the costs of prohibition because of their "economic dependence" on drug laws; these people profit financially from drug laws and are unwilling to undergo the economic "withdrawal" that would be caused by their repeal. . . .

The Harmful Effects of Drug Laws on Drug Users

At least part of the motivation for drug prohibition is that drug use is thought to harm those who engage in this activity. A perceived benefit of drug prohibition is that fewer people will engage in self-harming conduct than would in the absence of prohibition. While this contention will not be disputed here, there is another dimension of the issue of harm to drug users that may seem obvious to most when pointed out, but nonetheless is generally ignored in policy discussions of drug prohibition. To what degree are the harms of drug use caused not by intoxicating drugs, but by the fact that such drugs are illegal?

The most obvious harm to drug users caused by drug laws is the legal and physical jeopardy in which they are placed. Imprisonment must generally be considered a harm to the person imprisoned or it would hardly be an effective deterrent. To deter certain conduct it is advocated that we punish—in the sense of forcibly inflicting unpleasantness upon—those who engage in this conduct. In so doing it is hoped that people will be discouraged from engaging in the prohibited conduct.

But what about those who are not discouraged and who engage in such conduct anyway? Does the practice of punishing these persons make life better or worse for them? The answer is clear. As harmful as using drugs may be to someone, being imprisoned makes matters much worse.

Normally when considering matters of legality, we are not concerned about whether a law punishes a lawbreaker and makes him worse off. Indeed, normally such punishment is deliberately imposed on the lawbreaker to protect someone else whom we consider to be completely innocent—like the victim (or potential victim) of rape, robbery, or murder. We are therefore quite willing to harm the lawbreaker to protect the innocent. In other words, the objects of these laws are the victims, the subjects of these laws are the criminal[s].

Drug laws are different in this respect from many other criminal laws. With drug prohibition we are supposed to be concerned with the well-being of prospective drug users. So the object of drug laws—the persons whom drug laws are supposed to "protect"—are often the same persons who are the subject of drug laws. Whenever the object of a law is also its subject, however, a problem arises. The means chosen for benefiting prospective drug users seriously harms those who still use drugs and does so in ways that drugs alone cannot: by punishing drug users over and above the harmful effects of drug use. And the harm done by drug prohibition to drug users goes beyond the direct effects of punishment.

DRUG LAWS RAISE THE PRICE OF DRUGS TO USERS

Illegalization makes the prices of drugs rise. By increasing scarcity, the confiscation and destruction of drugs causes the price of the prohibited good to rise. And by increasing the risk to those who manufacture and sell, drug laws raise the cost of production and distribution, necessitating higher prices that reflect a "risk premium." (Price increases will not incur indefinitely, however, because at some level higher prices will induce more production.) Like the threat of punishment, higher prices may very well discourage some from using drugs who would otherwise do so. This is, in fact, the principal rationale for interdiction policies. But higher prices take their toll on those who are not deterred, and these adverse effects are rarely emphasized in discussions of drug laws.

Higher prices require higher income by users. If users cannot earn enough by legal means to pay higher prices, then they may be induced to engage in illegal conduct—theft, burglary, robbery—that they would not otherwise engage in. The increased harm caused to the victims of these crimes will be discussed below as a cost inflicted by drug laws on the general public. Of relevance here is the adverse effects that drug laws have on the life of drug users. By raising the costs of drugs, drug laws breed criminality. They induce some drug users who would not otherwise have contemplated criminal conduct to develop into the kind of people who are willing to commit crimes against others.

LEGALIZATION WOULD NOT INCREASE ACCESS TO DRUGS

Would drugs be more available once prohibition is repealed? It is hard to imagine drugs being more available than they are today. Despite efforts to stem their flow, drugs are accessible to anyone who wants them. In a recent government-sponsored survey of high school seniors, 55 percent said it would be "easy" for them to obtain cocaine, and 85 percent said it would be "easy" for them to obtain marijuana. In our inner-cities, access to drugs is especially easy, and the risk of arrest has proven to have a negligible deterrent effect. What would change under decriminalization is not so much drug availability as the conditions under which drugs would be available. Without prohibition, providing help to drug abusers who wanted to kick their habits would be easier because the money now being squandered on law enforcement could be used for preventive social programs and treatment.

American Civil Liberties Union, http://www.legalize-usa.org/documents/HTML/aclu.htm.

Higher prices can also make drug use more hazardous for users. Intravenous injection, for example, is more popular in countries where the high drug prices caused by prohibition give rise to the most "efficient" means of ingesting the drug. In countries where opiates are legal, the principal methods of consumption are inhaling the fumes of heated drugs or snorting. While physical dependence may result from either of these methods, neither is as likely as intravenous injections to result in an overdose. And consumption by injection can cause other health problems as well. For example: "Heroin use causes hepatitis only if injected, and causes collapsed veins and embolisms only if injected intravenously."

DRUG LAWS MAKE DRUG USERS BUY FROM CRIMINALS

Drug laws attempt to prohibit the use of substances that some people wish to consume. Thus because the legal sale of drugs is prohibited, people who still wish to use drugs are forced to do business with the kind of people who are willing to make and sell drugs in spite of the risk of punishment. Their dealings must be done away from the police. This puts users in great danger of physical harm in two ways.

First, they are likely to be the victims of crime. I would estimate that approximately half the murder cases I prosecuted were "drug related" in the sense that the victim was killed because it was thought he had either drugs or money from the sale of drugs. Crimes are also committed against persons who seek out criminals from whom to purchase prohibited drugs. These kinds of cases are brought to the attention of the authorities when the victim's body is found. A robbery of a drug user or dealer is hardly likely to be reported to the police.

Second, users are forced to rely upon criminals to regulate the quality and strength of the drugs they buy. No matter how carefully they measure their dosages, an unexpectedly potent supply may result in an overdose. And if the drug user is suspected to be a police informant, the dosage may deliberately be made potent by the supplier.

Drug laws make some comparatively benign intoxicating drugs—like opiates—artificially scarce and thereby create a powerful (black) market incentive for clandestine chemists to develop alternative "synthetic" drugs that can be made more cheaply and with less risk of detection by law enforcement. The hallucinogen, phencyclidine hydrochloride—or "PCP"—is one drug that falls into this category. Some of these substitute drugs may turn out to be far more dangerous than the substances they replace, both to the user and to others.

Drug Laws Criminalize Users

Prohibition automatically makes drug users into "criminals." While this point would seem too obvious to merit discussion, the effects of criminalization can be subtle and hidden. Criminalized drug users may not be able to obtain legitimate employment. This increases still further the likelihood that the artificially high prices of illicit drugs will lead drug users to engage in criminal conduct to obtain income. It is difficult to overestimate the harm caused by forcing drug users into a life of crime. Once this threshold is crossed, there is often no return. Such a choice would not be nearly so compelling if prohibited substances were legal.

Further, criminalization increases the hold that law enforcement agents have on drug users. This hold permits law enforcement agents to extort illegal payments from users or to coerce them into serving as informants who must necessarily engage in risky activity against others. Thus illegalization both motivates and enables the police to inflict harm on drug users in ways that would be impossible in the absence of the leverage provided by drug laws.

In sum, drug laws harm users of drugs well beyond any harm caused by drug use itself, and this extra harm is an unavoidable consequence of using legal means to prevent people from engaging in activity they deem desirable. While law enforcement efforts typically cause harm to criminals who victimize others, such effects are far more problematic with laws whose stated goals include helping the very people that the legal means succeed in harming. Support for drug laws in the face of those harms is akin to saying that we have to punish, criminalize, poison, rob, and murder drug users to save them from the harmful consequences of using intoxicating drugs.

To avoid these consequences, some have proposed abolishing laws against personal use of certain drugs, while continuing to ban the manufacture and sale of these substances. However, only the first and last of the five adverse consequences of drug prohibition just discussed result directly from punishing and criminalizing users. The other three harms to the user result indirectly from punishing those who manufacture and sell drugs. Decriminalizing the use of drugs would undoubtedly be an improvement over the status quo, but the remaining restrictions on manufacturing and sale would continue to cause serious problems for drug users beyond the problems caused by drug use itself.

As long as force is used to minimize drug use, these harms are unavoidable. They are caused by (1) the use of force (the legal means) to inflict pain on users, thereby directly harming them; and (2) the dangerous and criminalizing black market in drugs that results from efforts to stop some from making and selling a product others wish to consume. There is nothing that more enlightened law enforcement personnel or a more efficient administrative apparatus can do to prevent these effects from occurring. But, as the next section reveals, enlightened law enforcement personnel or an efficient administrative apparatus will not come from employing legal force to prevent adults from engaging in consensual activity.

THE HARMFUL EFFECTS OF DRUG LAWS ON THE GENERAL PUBLIC
The harmful side effects of drug laws are not limited to drug users. This section highlights the various harms that drug laws

inflict on the general public. There is an old saying in the criminal courts that is particularly apt here: "What goes around, comes around." In an effort to inflict pain on drug users, drug laws inflict considerable costs on nonusers as well.

The most obvious cost of drug prohibition is the expenditure of scarce resources to enforce drug laws—resources that can thus not be used to enforce other laws or be allocated to other productive activities outside of law enforcement.

Every dollar spent to punish a drug user or seller is a dollar that cannot be spent collecting restitution from a robber. Every hour spent investigating a drug user or seller is an hour that could have been used to find a missing child. Every trial held to prosecute a drug user or seller is court time that could be used to prosecute a rapist in a case that might otherwise have been plea bargained. These and countless other expenditures are the "opportunity costs" of drug prohibition.

INCREASED CRIME

By artificially raising the price of illicit drugs and thereby forcing drug users to obtain large sums of money, drug laws create powerful incentives to commit property and other profitable crimes. And the interaction between drug users and criminally inclined drug sellers presents users with many opportunities to become involved in all types of illegal conduct.

Finally, usually neglected in discussions of drugs and crime are the numerous "drug-related" robberies and murders (sometimes of innocent parties wrongly thought to have drugs) that the constant interaction between users and criminal sellers creates. Drug dealers and buyers are known to carry significant quantities of either cash or valuable substances. They must deliberately operate outside the vision of the police. They can rely only on self-help for personal protection.

Many drug-law users speculate quite freely about the intangible "adverse effects of drug use on a society." They are strangely silent, however, about how the fabric of society is affected by the increase in both property crimes and crimes of violence caused by drug laws. . . .

CURING THE DRUG-LAW ADDICTION

An addiction to drug laws is caused by an inadequate understanding of individual rights and the vital role such rights play in deciding matters of legality. As a result, policies are implemented that cause serious harm to the very individuals whom these policies were devised to help and to the general public.

If the rights of individuals to choose how to use their person and possessions are fully respected, there is no guaranty that they will exercise their rights wisely. Some may mistakenly choose the path of finding happiness in a bottle or in a vial. Others may wish to help these people by persuading them of their folly. But we must not give in to the powerful temptation to grant some the power to impose their consumptive preferences on others by force. This power—the "essence" of drug laws—is not only "addictive" once it is tasted, it carries with it one of the few guaranties in life: the guaranty of untold corruption and human misery.

"More people would use [drugs]
under almost any conceivable version
of legalization than is true today,
and more would use compulsively
and abusively."

LEGALIZING DRUGS WOULD INCREASE ADDICTION

Erich Goode

In the following viewpoint, Erich Goode argues that drug legalization would increase drug use and addiction. According to Goode, the threat of arrest acts a strong deterrent against drug use. If drug use carried no criminal penalties, more people would be tempted to experiment with drugs. Among these, many would become hooked on highly pleasurable drugs such as cocaine. Erich Goode is the author of the book *Between Politics and Reason*, from which the following viewpoint has been excerpted.

As you read, consider the following questions:
1. According to Goode, how do drug prohibitionists and drug legalizers differ in their views of human nature?
2. Why does cocaine possess the greatest potential for dependence, in the author's analysis?
3. What evidence does Goode provide to support his claim that greater availability of drugs leads to more use?

Excerpted from Erich Goode, *Between Politics and Reason*. Copyright ©1997 by St. Martin's Press, Inc. Reprinted with permission of Bedford/St. Martin's Press, Inc.

All predictions of what is likely to happen under certain conditions are based on specific assumptions about human nature—a general theory of behavior, if you will. [Drug] legalizers and [drug] prohibitionists hold contrasting sets of assumptions about human nature; perhaps it will be worthwhile to look at them under a microscope.

The legalizers see human nature as basically rational, sane, temperate, and wise. As stated by Gazzaniga, "Inform a normally intelligent group of people about the tangible hazards of using a particular substance and the vast majority of them will simply stop." That is, the *reason* why drug abuse will not rise sharply under legalization is that most people are cautious and not willing to take risks; since currently illegal drugs entail a certain likelihood of harm, it is extremely unlikely that they will be taken up by many people who are not currently already using. In contrast, one of the reasons that prohibitionists cite in support of their argument is their assumption . . . that many people are not nearly so rational and moderate in their behavior as the legalizers believe. Many, many Americans will experiment with and use heroin and cocaine, the prohibitionists believe; of this total, a substantial proportion will become compulsively involved with them to the point of abuse and addiction. The reason why this will happen, the prohibitionists believe, is that many of us are willing to take dangerous risks; they feel that a substantial number of us believe that bad things happen to *other* people but not to *us*, that we, somehow, are somehow lucky enough to do potentially dangerous things, yet not get hurt. A lot more people are reckless risk-takers than the legalizers think, the prohibitionists argue. In fact, they say, this is precisely the reason why we have criminal laws outlawing certain activities: By introducing the risk of arrest, society can dissuade the *slightly* foolhardy from engaging in high-risk activities, leaving only a fairly *small* number of *very* foolhardy souls who will be willing to do so.

APOLLONIANS AND DIONYSIANS

Many decades ago, Ruth Benedict published a classic in the anthropological literature, *Patterns of Culture*. In that book, she made a distinction between two approaches to life—the *Apollonian* and the *Dionysian*. In the ancient Greek and Roman religions, Apollo was the god of poetry, music, light, healing, and manly beauty, while Dionysus was the god of fertility, wine, and drama. Hence, the Apollonian approach to life is a "classical," measured, graceful, traditional, rational way of living, while the Dionysian approach is pleasure-seeking, lustful, hedonistic, selfish, risk-taking, even violent and dangerous. Some cultures stand more at the Apollonian end of this spectrum, while others stand at the Dionysian end. Likewise, some people are more Apollonian, others are more Dionysian. The [drug] legalizer's general theory of human nature (or, at least, the American version of it) is Apollonian; the prohibitionist's is Dionysian.

In my view, the argument between the criminalizers (who see human nature as closer to the Dionysian pole) and the legalizers (who see it as more Apollonian) is misplaced. To put it another way, both sides are partly right—and partly wrong. In fact, while most Americans are not Dionysian risk-takers, this is irrelevant. The crucial issue is not the orientation of most Americans, but the orientation of a minority. There are enough Dionysians in this society who, under the right social and legal conditions, would be inclined to experiment with drugs and seriously disrupt the lives of the rest of us. In spite of the practical, hard-working, sober veneer of most Americans, many of us are a great deal more Dionysian than we are willing to admit. There are many among us who want to drive fast cars, get intoxicated on psychoactive drugs, engage in a variety of sexual adventures, neglect our workaday and family obligations, eat fattening foods without restraint, dance until dawn, and commit a wide range of criminal acts, but who are afraid of the consequences—social, monetary, and, for some of these actions, legal consequences. The removal of legal penalties outlawing one of them—getting intoxicated on drugs—would make drugs more attractive to a substantial number of Americans. My contention is that the threat of arrest and imprisonment is one of the mechanisms that keep the wilder side of the *moderate* Dionysians (if such a creature is not a contradiction in terms) in check, while the small minority of *extreme* Dionysians remain undeterred by any manner of risk, legal or otherwise.

But here's an extremely important point: The legalizers are correct in assuming that *most* of us are *not* true Dionysians. Most Americans would *not* experiment with heroin or cocaine, and, of those who would, most would *not* become unwisely and abusively involved with them. There is almost *no* chance that, under legalization, heroin or cocaine would ever become as popular as cigarettes or alcohol. The vast majority of Americans would shun the recreational use of the currently illegal drugs, and the vast majority of those who would use them would be temperate and moderate in their use. Comments one critic of the current policy, "while certain drugs can produce physical dependence, most individuals will not willingly take those drugs, even after experiencing their effects." Still, this is irrelevant. What is important is that *more* people would use under almost any conceivable version of legalization than is true today, and more would use compulsively and abusively.

RISK VERSUS HARM

I do believe that most people do not want to harm themselves. I believe that the evidence shows that, however inaccurately, people generally do calculate cost and benefit before engaging in certain actions. (Indeed, this is one of the reasons behind enacting and enforcing criminal laws.) But risk is not the same thing as *harm*; risk entails taking chances—it is not a guarantee of being harmed. A certain proportion of motorcyclists refuse to wear helmets. For most of them who take that risk, not wearing helmets will make no difference to their life or limb, because most will not get into a serious accident. The same applies to motorists who do not want to wear a seat belt; for most of them, not wearing a seat belt is in fact *not* harmful. However, harm enters into the picture not in each and every case but in the overall picture. Injury and fatality statistics are very clear about this: You are *more* likely to be seriously injured and die if you do not wear a helmet or a seat belt. *Some* (not all, not even most) motorcyclists are harmed because they didn't wear a helmet; *some* motorists are harmed because they didn't wear a seat belt. The law convinces a very substantial proportion of motorcyclists and motorists to wear these protective devices; even more persuasive than a law by itself is a law with real penalties and vigorous enforcement.

Again, it is simply irrelevant to argue that most "normally intelligent people" will give up an activity if they are aware of the "tangible hazards" of an activity or substance. The fact is, the risk an activity entails is not always clear-cut, obvious, or immediately apparent. Indeed, the danger in question may *never* manifest itself because, once again, risk is a statistical, not an absolute, affair. Most people are not harmed *at all* by a great many very risky activities. The two crucial issues are, first, the absolute number who are harmed, not the proportion, and, second, the number who are persuaded not to take a given physical risk because of an entirely separate risk—the likelihood of arrest. In my view, if that second risk were removed, a substantial number of people would engage in harmful, abusive drug taking. (Why do the legalizers emphasize the dissuasive power of physical risk but ignore the power of the threat of arrest and imprisonment?) Not a majority, not even remotely close to . . . tens of millions of Americans, but a substantial number. Seeing the American population as far more Dionysian than the legalizers do leads me to conclude that legalization will result in a significant rise in drug use and abuse. . . .

THE ROLE OF REINFORCEMENT

With respect to drugs,"reinforcement" refers, roughly, to how enjoyable a substance is, its capacity to deliver an orgasm-like jolt or "rush" of unmodified, undiluted, unsocialized pleasure. "Reinforcement" refers to the reward an organism achieves upon taking the drug and the commitment it has to continue taking it. To put the matter in more formal terms, the more reinforcing a drug, the harder an organism will work to continue taking it. The reinforcing potential of drugs can be determined even among nonhuman organisms; rats, mice, and monkeys find cocaine (and, to a lesser degree, heroin and amphetamine) immensely pleasurable; they will press a bar hundreds of times in order to receive a single dose of the drug. In a laboratory situation, they will take it as much as they can and will even risk their lives to do so. They will take cocaine in preference to food and water, and will even kill themselves, self-administering cocaine. Moreover, if they have taken cocaine over a period of time and the drug is suddenly discontinued, they will continue doing whatever they did previously that rewarded them with doses of cocaine, but now go unrewarded, for a longer period of time than for any other drug, including heroin. Psychologists regard whatever produces such slow-to-extinguish previously rewarded behavior as extremely reinforcing.

In this respect, then, cocaine stands at the top of all widely used psychoactive drugs; it possesses the greatest *immediate sensual appeal*; this means that previously inexperienced subjects who are administered a range of drugs without knowing what they are being given are most likely to say they liked cocaine and most likely to say they want to take it again. Most pharmacologists and psychologists now argue that psychological reinforcement, not physical dependence, is the key to dependence. Drugs that are highly pleasurable in a direct, immediate, sensual way are most likely to produce addict-like behavior in users, *whether or not* these drugs produce a literal, physical addiction, that is, withdrawal symptoms. In this respect, then, among all widely used psychoactive drugs, cocaine possesses the greatest potential for producing dependence. . . .

Other things being equal, the pharmacological properties of cocaine (and, to a much lesser extent, heroin) should lead anyone to predict an increase in use. There is, in other words, sufficient ground for genuine concern when it comes to sharply reducing the cost and increasing the availability of cocaine, given its intrinsically pleasure-inducing and reinforcing property. A great deal of contrary evidence would have to be marshaled to convince evidence-minded observers that cocaine abuse would not rise sharply under legalization—and, as yet, no such evidence has been forthcoming. In the absence of such evidence, most of us will have to remain convinced that, in the words of John Kaplan, legalization "ignores basic pharmacology." It almost defies logic to assume that, when criminal penalties are removed, the use of an entire array of pleasurable, highly reinforcing drugs will not rise significantly.

FREQUENCIES OF USE

What direct evidence do we have that bears on the impact of legalization on drug use? Contrarily, what evidence bears on the impact of the criminalization of drugs and enforcement of the drug laws on use? Does drug use/abuse rise when drugs are legalized and fall when they are criminalized? Or, as the legalizers assume, does law enforcement have little or no impact on the incidence and volume of use? What circumstances make drugs more, or less, available? Is there a variety of controls which influence use, and not merely legal ones? What does the use picture under nonlegal controls tell us about the impact of legal controls?

We already know that national alcohol prohibition in the United States (1920–1933) did discourage use: Fewer Americans drank, and fewer contracted cirrhosis of the liver during Prohibition than before and afterward. (Prohibition brought about a number of other changes, as we saw, but they are separate from the issue of volume of alcohol consumption.) We also know that the partial decriminalization of small quantities of marijuana in nine states of the United States has not resulted in a significant increase in the use of this drug. It is entirely possible that marijuana is a case apart from cocaine and heroin. At any rate, cocaine and heroin are the drugs most Americans fear and worry about the most. A number of observers have endorsed the legalization of marijuana and yet oppose the legalization of hard drugs such as heroin and/or cocaine. And the Dutch policy (often mistakenly referred to as "legalization") is based on making a sharp distinction between "soft" drugs such as marijuana and hashish and "hard" drugs such as cocaine and heroin. Hence, the case for or against heroin and/or cocaine legalization will have to be made separately from the case for or against the legalization of marijuana.

Several pieces of evidence suggest (but do not definitively demonstrate) that when the *availability* of certain drugs increases, their *use* increases as well. It has been something of a cliché among legalizers that criminalization doesn't work. Look around you, they say. Go to certain neighborhoods, and see drugs openly sold on the street. Drugs are getting into the hands of addicts and abusers right now. How could the situation be any worse under legalization? Those who want to use are already using; selling drugs to addicts, abusers, and users legally would not change anything, they say.

EXPERIMENTS IN DISASTER

The ventures of Switzerland, England, the Netherlands, and Italy into drug legalization have had disastrous consequences. Switzerland's "Needle Park," touted as a way to restrict a few hundred heroin addicts to a small area, turned into a grotesque tourist attraction of 20,000 heroin addicts and junkies that had to be closed down before it infected the city of Zurich. England's foray into allowing any doctor to prescribe heroin quickly was curbed as heroin use increased.

In the Netherlands, anyone over age 17 can drop into a marijuana "coffee shop" and pick types of marijuana like one might choose flavors of ice cream. Adolescent pot use there jumped nearly 200% while it was dropping by 66% in the U.S. . . .

Italy infrequently is mentioned by advocates of legalization, despite its lenient drug laws. Personal possession of small amounts of drugs has not been a crime in Italy since 1975, other than a brief period of recriminalization between 1990 and 1993. (Even then, Italy permitted an individual to possess one dose of a drug.) Under decriminalization, possession of two to three doses of drugs such as heroin generally was exempt from criminal sanction. Today, Italy has 300,000 addicts, the highest rate of heroin addiction in Europe. Seventy percent of all AIDS cases in Italy are attributable to drug use.

Joseph A. Califano Jr., *USA Today*, March 1997.

The fallacy in this line of reasoning is that, currently, under our punitive policy, addicts and abusers are *not* using as much as they would like. Under almost any currently proposed legalization plan, the currently illegal drugs would be more available; if that were so, current abusers and addicts would use a great deal *more* cocaine and heroin than they do now. The fact that we can look around on the streets of the country's largest cities and see drug selling taking place means next to nothing. The fact is, there is the "hassle factor" to consider. Addicts are *pulled into* use by the fact that they enjoy getting high, but they are *pushed away* from use by the fact that they have to commit crime to do so. Street crime is difficult, risky, and dangerous; use is held down by that fact. If drugs were less of a "hassle" to obtain, the majority of addicts and abusers would use it more. The vast majority of heroin and cocaine abusers want to get high, are forced to commit a great deal of crime to do so, and are not getting high as often as they want because their drugs of choice are too expensive, and the crimes they commit are too much of a "hassle," for them to use as much as they want. Mark Moore refers to this as the "search time" for illegal drugs; says Moore, as "search time" goes up, demand decreases. Careful ethnographic and interview studies of street addicts and abusers have shown that getting high—not mere maintenance—is their prime motivation. Most are not technically addicted, their day-to-day use varies enormously, and most would use *much more* frequently if they could. In this sense, then, the drug laws and their enforcement have cut down on the *volume* of drug use among a substantial proportion—very possibly a majority—of our heaviest users and abusers. Again, the distinction between relative and absolute deterrence comes into play here; these addicts and abusers use a *substantial quantity* of illegal drugs—but a great deal less than they would if these drugs were legal or freely available to them. Ironically, the drug laws are *most* effective against the drug use of the *heaviest* users, those, who, moreover, are arrested the most.

AVAILABILITY WOULD INCREASE USE

Goldstein and Kalant base their opposition to legalization on the observation that use is directly related to availability, and availability can be influenced by a variety of controls, including criminalization and cost. Under all legalization plans, the currently illegal drugs would be sold or dispensed at a fraction of their present price. Indeed, that is the advantage of this plan, say its supporters, because the high cost of drugs leads to crime which, in turn, leads to a panoply of social harms, costs, and problems. But Goldstein and Kalant argue exactly the opposite: that the high cost of the illegal drugs is *specifically* what keeps their use down. If drugs were to be sold or dispensed at low prices, use would almost inevitably rise—in all likelihood, dramatically. This relationship is demonstrated, they say, with a variety of drugs in a variety of settings. For instance, as measured by constant dollars, cost and the per-capita consumption of alcohol—and the rate of cirrhosis of the liver—were almost perfectly correlated in a negative fashion in the Canadian province of Ontario between 1928 and 1974: During periods when the price of alcohol was low, the use of alcohol was relatively high; when the price of alcohol was high, use was relatively low. Price and use were mirror reflections of one another. In addition, observe Goldstein and Kalant, the purchase of cigarettes, and therefore smoking, varies directly and negatively with the level of taxation on cigarettes: The higher the taxes on cigarettes, the lower their sales. "These data suggest that anything making drugs less expensive, such as legal sale at lower prices, would result in substantial increases in use and in the harmful consequences of heavy use."

There are two additional pieces of evidence bearing on the relationship between the availability of psychoactive drugs and their use: first, the immense rise in the use of and addiction to narcotics among servicemen stationed in Vietnam, and the sharp decline in use and addiction upon their return to the United States; and second, the higher rates of certain types of psychoactive drug use among physicians and other health workers—who have greater access to drugs—than is true of the population as a whole.

THE CASE OF THE MILITARY IN VIETNAM

Robins reports that almost half of a sample of U.S. military servicemen serving in Vietnam in the 1970s had tried one or more narcotic drugs (opium, heroin, and/or morphine), and 20 percent were addicted to opiates. Prior to their arrival in Vietnam, however, only a small fraction had ever been addicted, and after their return to the United States, use and addiction fell back to their pre-Vietnam levels. (This study cross-checked self-reports on drug use with urine tests; hence, we can have a high degree of confidence in the answers on use and addiction.) This study's findings are significant for at least two reasons.

First, the fact that the vast majority of addicted returning veterans discontinued their dependence on and use of narcotics on their own, without going through a formal therapeutic program, has major implications for the study of drug treatment. And second, and more central for our purposes, the fact that use and addiction increased massively in Vietnam, where drugs were freely available (although technically illegal), and returned to their previous, extremely low levels when these veterans returned to the United States, gives us a glimpse of what may happen under legalization. The fact that 95 percent of those who became addicted in Vietnam had not been addicted in the United States, and a similar 95 percent who became addicted in Vietnam ceased their addiction when they returned to the United States, tells us that there must have been something about the conditions that prevailed in Vietnam that *encouraged* use and addiction, as well as something about those conditions that prevailed in the United States that *discouraged* them. Some observers have attributed the high levels of drug abuse that prevailed in Vietnam to the combat stress that these servicemen experienced, but it is unlikely that this is the whole explanation. It seems almost *incontestable* that the greater availability of drugs in Vietnam induced an enormous number of servicemen to use, and become addicted to, narcotics who otherwise would not have become involved. Their low level of narcotic addiction in the United States, both before and after their Vietnam experience, was almost certainly influenced by the fact that opiates are illegal here.

PHYSICIAN DRUG USE

There are three aspects of physician drug use that are significantly higher than is true for the population at large.

First, as a number of studies have shown, the fact that recreational drug use among medical students and younger physicians is strikingly higher than among their age peers in the general population, again, suggests that availability is related to the likelihood of use. In one study, 73 percent of medical students had at least one recreational experience with at least one illegal psychoactive drug. In comparison, for 18- to 25-year-olds in the general population at roughly the same time, the figure was 55 percent, and for 26- to 34-year-olds, it was 62 percent. For cocaine, the comparable figures were 39 percent for medical students and, in the general population, 18 percent for 18- to 25-year-olds and 26 percent for 26- to 34-year-olds.

Second, rates of *self-medication* among physicians are strikingly higher than is true among the general population. In the study of physician drug use cited above, four out of 10 physicians (42 percent) said that they had treated themselves with one or more psychoactive drugs one or more times, and 7 percent said that they had done so on 60 or more occasions; one-third of medical students had done so once or more, and 5 percent had done so on 60 or more occasions. This represents an extraordinarily high rate of self-medication with psychoactive drugs.

And third, the proportion of physicians reporting drug *dependence* is extraordinarily high—3 percent of physicians and 5 percent of medical students said that they were currently dependent on a psychoactive drug, far higher than for the population as a whole. Other surveys have produced similar results. While occupational stress, once again, has often been cited as the culprit which causes high levels of physician drug use, abuse, and dependence, as with the Vietnam situation, it is difficult to deny that *availability* plays a substantial role. And it is greater availability that every proposed legalization plan offers; to the extent that some "legalization" proposal does *not* offer availability, then clearly, at that point, as with the current system, illegal market processes take over.

"Government must significantly expand its drug enforcement efforts, putting many more police on the streets, building more prisons, and expanding the use of . . . military forces in demolishing crack houses."

THE GOVERNMENT SHOULD DIRECT ITS RESOURCES TOWARD LAW ENFORCEMENT

Michael DeCourcy Hinds

Michael DeCourcy Hinds, vice president and executive editor of Public Agenda, a nonprofit, nonpartisan research and education organization based in New York, contends in the following viewpoint that increased law enforcement measures are needed to combat the problem of drug abuse and addiction. He asserts that tougher penalties for drug lords, dealers, and users—along with stronger efforts to seal international borders from drug smuggling—will help eradicate the problem of drugs.

As you read, consider the following questions:

1. What international measures should the government take against drugs, according to Public Agenda?
2. According to the author, what can communities do to prevent illegal drug use?
3. How can law enforcement make sure that drug dealing doesn't pay, in the author's view?

Nearly 70 percent of the cocaine sold on American streets comes from drug cartels in Cali, Colombia. Organized Mexican gangs help transport the cocaine, with a street value of $6,000 per pound, across the U.S. border in secret compartments of thousands of vehicles. The operators of this network are "a new breed of international organized criminals whose power and influence make America's mafia look like child's play," Thomas A. Constantine, administrator of the Drug Enforcement Administration, told Congress in June 1996.

Constantine was testifying about a just-completed investigation documenting the domination of the U.S. drug trade by Colombian and Mexican wholesalers, who, in turn, supply American drug dealers on the street. By the end of the eight-month investigation in May 1996, police had arrested 156 people, and had seized six tons of cocaine and $17 million in drug profits. The international investigation, dubbed Operation Zorro II, serves as a model of cooperation, involving law enforcement officials from 11 federal agencies and 42 state and local agencies.

A CRIMINAL PROBLEM

Illegal drugs, by definition, are a criminal problem, one that will only worsen without a commitment to substantially increase enforcement, according to supporters [of tougher law enforcement measures]. In this view, a tough, uncompromising response to the illegal drug problem is required because Americans are deeply concerned that drugs are destructive to individuals and threaten our entire way of life. Government statistics indicate that our antidrug efforts over the past 20 years have produced significant success: more than a 50 percent drop in the number of people in every age group who try drugs or use them casually. But current levels of enforcement and existing community antidrug campaigns are not nearly enough. How else can one explain the vast quantities of drugs that daily slip into this country in cars driven by noncitizens? How else can one explain the public sale of drugs on American streets everywhere? And how else can one explain the proliferation of crack houses, where everyone, including the police, knows that cocaine is sold to a traffic jam of addicts?

A ROLE FOR EVERYONE

Americans must make drug eradication a top national priority, with innovative strategies to break every link in the chain of drug production and distribution at the international, national, and community levels.

Internationally, the U.S. should increase economic assistance to help other governments eradicate drugs from their farms, factories, and economies. U.S. military forces should cooperate with foreign governments in destroying the drug factories and prosecuting the drug lords. As a last resort—especially when a foreign government has been corrupted by drug money, as is apparently the case in Colombia—the U.S. should be willing to intervene on its own, much as it did in 1989 by removing Panama's General Manuel Noriega and imprisoning him for allowing drug traffickers to operate from his nation with impunity. The government must also seal our leaky international borders against drugs, expanding border patrols on land and sea and in the air.

On a national level, we must strengthen criminal laws so that law enforcement officials can do the job Americans want them to do. Government must significantly expand its drug enforcement efforts, putting many more police on the streets, building more prisons, and expanding the use of the National Guard and perhaps other military forces in demolishing crack houses and protecting communities. The nation must deal strictly with drug dealers and drug users alike, strengthening laws so that offenders are punished more severely and drug profits are seized.

But getting serious about eradicating drugs means much more than increasing the government's role. Drugs have saturated our communities so thoroughly that we cannot expect the government alone to solve the problem—as individuals and members of community organizations, we must take responsibility for stopping drug use and sales in every community. For our own good, we must insist that schools conduct locker-room searches, that employers conduct random drug tests, and that police help communities develop neighborhood watch patrols. The nation's message must be simple and unambiguous: zero tolerance for illegal drug use.

KEEP DRUGS OUT

The war on drugs, in this view, should not be just a federal and state responsibility but also a local effort in every American city, town, suburb, and rural area. For example, urban communities that have succeeded in fighting drugs often combine two strategies: 1) antidrug campaigns, in which citizens make it clear that they will not tolerate drug dealing in their neighborhood; and 2) community policing, which generally involves a municipality assigning more police to foot patrols, regular beats, and community meetings. In Philadelphia, where the police work side by side with community group members, the crime rate declined by 20 percent between 1989 and 1993. In one formerly drug-infested neighborhood called Mantua, the combined strategy resulted in a whopping 40 percent decrease in crime during those years. Leading the community effort is a citizen's group called Mantua Against Drugs. MAD, as it's called, has become a national model for citizen involvement in the war on drugs.

WHAT CAN BE DONE?

- Seal our international borders to illegal drugs and demand international cooperation in breaking up drug cartels. If necessary, impose stiff economic sanctions against drug-exporting countries. As a last resort, especially in cases where drug profits have corrupted a foreign government, use military force to destroy drug factories and cartel strongholds.

- Substantially increase funding for enforcement. Put more police on the streets, expand border patrols, and strengthen state and federal drug enforcement efforts, including surveillance and undercover programs.

- Have police help citizens develop antidrug campaigns and patrols to protect their communities.

- Expand canine sniff searches and random testing for illegal drugs to all schools and workplaces. Make public benefits like welfare and unemployment compensation contingent on passing drug tests. Encourage parents of teenagers to use newly available at-home drug tests.

- Impose mandatory minimum prison sentences on drug users and dealers—most drug offenders now serve only a third of their prison terms.

- Support the investment in effective enforcement by building more prisons.

- Destroy drug dealers' business by expanding seizures of their property and drug profits.

Public Agenda, *National Issues Forums: Illegal Drugs: What Should We Do Now?* 1997.

Wearing white construction helmets and armed only with bullhorns, the mostly elderly men and women of MAD occupy street corners and block off access to tenements where drug dealers operate. "We get neighbors to know it's their responsibility to take the lead in this," said C.B. Kimmins, MAD's executive director. "We get in the drug dealers' faces, telling them to get out of the neighborhood. We're not vigilantes, but we don't back down." Working with police, MAD has closed down more crack houses than its members can count.

Make Sure Dealing Drugs Doesn't Pay

Too often, drug dealers are back on the street the day after they are arrested. And when they are sent to prison, they usually keep their illegal drug profits and often serve only a portion of their sentence. To deter drug trafficking, government must ensure that drug dealing is a losing, dead-end business, in this view.

Mandatory minimum sentences, which specify the minimum period of incarceration for some crimes, should be applied to all drug-related crimes—and the minimum sentences should be lengthened to make prison a more effective deterrent.

Seizing drug profits is another way to deter these crimes, as well as a way to offset some enforcement costs. In 1995, for example, federal prosecutors seized more than $150 million in drug profits from Swiss bank accounts of a single Colombian family, the Nassers, who had exported an estimated 27 tons of cocaine and 1,500 tons of marijuana to the U.S. since 1976. Since the late 1980s, U.S. seizures of drug traffickers' assets have averaged $600 million annually, according to government statistics.

[This approach] supports city and state efforts to make greater use of seizure and forfeiture laws at the local level. In Detroit, for example, police seize the automobiles of drivers who cruise through neighborhoods to buy drugs. To redeem their vehicles, drivers have to pay $950; the program generated more than $630,000 in 1995 and chased drug buyers out of city neighborhoods—now only 1 in 100 seized vehicles is owned by a repeat offender.

"If we don't deal with alcohol and
drug abuse and revamp our system
of crime and punishment, one of
every 20 Americans born in 1997
will spend some time in jail."

THE GOVERNMENT SHOULD DIRECT ITS RESOURCES TOWARD DRUG TREATMENT

Joseph A. Califano Jr.

In the following viewpoint, Joseph A. Califano challenges the notion that strict law enforcement measures will eliminate the problem of drug addiction. He maintains that a better solution is to provide treatment and job training for addicted inmates so that they can return to society as productive, law-abiding citizens. Califano is president of the National Center on Addiction and Substance Abuse at Columbia University, a think tank whose goals are to inform Americans of the economic and social costs of substance abuse; assess what works in prevention, treatment, and law enforcement; and remove the stigma of substance abuse.

As you read, consider the following questions:

1. According to the author, what percentage of people in jail are estimated to have a problem with drugs or alcohol?
2. How can treatment programs save money, in Califano's assessment?
3. On what basis does Califano call the present system of prison and punishment "insane public policy"?

Reprinted from Joseph A. Califano Jr., "Crime and Punishment—and Treatment, Too," published at www.casacolumbia.org/media/crime.htm, February 8, 1998, by permission of the author.

It's time to open—in the nation's prisons—a second front in the war on crime.

For two decades, we have been filling prisons with drug and alcohol abusers and addicts and, without treatment or training, returning them to society to resume the criminal activity spawned by their substance abuse. This is public policy crafted in the theater of the absurd.

Individuals who commit serious offenses such as drug dealing and violent and property crimes belong in prison. But it is just as much in the interest of the public safety to rehabilitate those who can be redeemed as it is to keep incorrigibles locked up.

THE SCOPE OF THE PROBLEM

More than 1.7 million people are behind bars in America: 1.6 million in state prisons and local jails, 100,000 in federal prisons. Eighty percent—1.4 million inmates—either violated drug or alcohol laws, were high at the time of their offense, stole property to buy drugs, have histories of drug and alcohol abuse and addiction, or share some mix of these characteristics. Among these 1.4 million inmates are the parents of 2.4 million children.

Two hundred thousand of these prisoners dealt drugs, but don't use them. The remaining 1.2 million are drug and alcohol abusers and addicts. Some would have committed their crimes regardless of their substance abuse. But hundreds of thousands are individuals whose core problem is the abuse and addiction that prompted their criminal activity. They would be law-abiding, taxpaying citizens and responsible parents if they lived sober lives.

SAVING MONEY WITH TREATMENT

The National Center on Addiction and Substance Abuse at Columbia University estimates that for an additional $6,500 a year, an inmate could be given intensive treatment, education and job training. Upon release, each one who worked at the average wage of a high school graduate for a year would return an investment of $68,000 in reduced criminal activity, savings on the costs of arrest, prosecution, incarceration and health care, and benefit to the economy. If all 1.2 million inmates with drug and alcohol problems got such treatment and training (cost: $7.8 billion) and only 10 percent became sober, working citizens (benefits: $8.256 billion), the investment would pay for itself within a year of work. Each subsequent year would provide billions more in savings and economic benefits.

The potential crime reduction is also big league. Expert estimates of crimes committed by the average drug addict range from 89 to 191 a year. At the conservative end, successfully treating and training just 10,000 drug addicts would eliminate 1 million crimes a year.

INSANE PUBLIC POLICY

After three years studying the relationship between prison inmates and substance abuse, I am convinced that the present system of prison and punishment only is insane public policy. Despite tougher sentencing laws, on average inmates are released in 18 months to four years. Even those convicted of such violent crimes as aggravated assault and robbery get out in three to four years.

Releasing drug and alcohol addicts and abusers without treatment or training is tantamount to visiting criminals on society. Releasing drug addicts is a government price support program for the illegal drug market. Temporarily housing such prisoners without treating and training them is a profligate use of public funds and the greatest missed opportunity to cut crime further.

TREATMENT MORE COST-EFFECTIVE THAN PRISON

[The Physician Leadership on National Drug Policy] contend[s] that medical care for addicts either on an out-patient or residential basis is cheaper than the $25,900 it costs annually to imprison a drug addict. It prices regular outpatient care at $1,800 to $2,500 a year, methadone maintenance at $3,900, and residential treatment at $4,400 to $6,800.

Lawrence M. O'Rourke, Sacramento Bee, March 24, 1998.

One of every 144 Americans is behind bars, one of every sixty men, one of every 14 black men. If we don't deal with alcohol and drug abuse and revamp our system of crime and punishment, one of every 20 Americans born in 1997 will spend some time in jail, including one of every 11 men and one of every four black men.

Politicians camouflage the failure of their punishment-only prison policy by snorting tough rhetoric. They talk and act as though the only people in prison are violent black crack addicts and incorrigible psychopaths like James Cagney in Public Enemy, as though treatment doesn't work and addiction is a moral failing that any individual can easily change.

FACING REALITY

The first step toward sensible criminal justice policy is to face reality. Prisons are wall to wall with drug and alcohol addicts and abusers. Appropriate substance abuse treatment has a higher success rate than many long-shot cancer therapies. (It could certainly help 20 percent of this population: that's a quarter of a million criminals who could be turned into law-abiding citizens and good parents.)

The common denominator among inmates is not race; it's drug and alcohol abuse. Though blacks are disproportionately represented in prison, essentially the same proportion (61 to 65 percent) of black, white, and Hispanic inmates are regular drug users. Alcohol is more tightly linked with violent crime than crack cocaine: in state prisons, 21 percent of criminals were high on alcohol alone at the time of their offenses; only 3 percent were high on crack or cocaine alone.

Each year the government builds more prisons and hires more prison guards. In effect, governors, presidents, and legislators keep saying, "If all the king's horses and all the king's men can't put Humpty Dumpty back together again, then give us more horses and give us more men."

We need a revolution in the way we think about prisons, crime and punishment in America. Our political leaders should put some common sense behind their tough talk by opening a second front in the war on crime with a heavy investment in treatment and training for the drug and alcohol abusers they have crammed into our prisons. If they do, the nation's streets will be safer, and the cost of law enforcement will be lower.

| "Given the dreadful health consequences associated with a lifetime of tobacco use, it is fair and in the public interest to do everything possible to restrict youth access to these products."

INCREASED REGULATION OF TOBACCO PRODUCTS WOULD REDUCE TEENAGE SMOKING

Richard B. Heyman

In 1995, the Food and Drug Administration (FDA), at the initiative of President Bill Clinton, proposed tobacco regulations that are intended to reduce teen smoking. The regulations, which have since passed but are facing challenges in the courts, eliminate cigarette vending machines, mail samplings and giveways, and brand-identified products such as clothing and sporting gear. In addition, billboards advertising tobacco products are prohibited near schools or playgrounds, other tobacco advertising is restricted to black and white text only, and no ads are permissible at sporting events. Richard B. Heyman claims in the following viewpoint that the FDA regulations are effective and reasonable ways to combat teen smoking. Heyman practices medicine in Cincinnati and is chairman of the Committee on Substance Abuse, American Academy of Pediatrics.

As you read, consider the following questions:

1. According to Heyman, what image of smokers has been created by the tobacco industry?
2. What evidence does the author provide to support his view that advertising encourages young people to smoke?

From Richard B. Heyman, "Teenage Smoking: More Laws Are Needed." This article appeared in the December 1995 issue of, and is reprinted with permission from, The World & I, a publication of The Washington Times Corporation, copyright ©1995.

"There they go again," says the tobacco industry. "We smokers have our rights," say the nicotine addicted. "Socialism is just around the corner," say the congressmen who are recipients of tobacco dollars.

We've heard it all, and as the voice of some 48,000 child health-care specialists nationwide, the American Academy of Pediatrics is tired of it. With the 1995 proposal to permit the Food and Drug Administration (FDA) to regulate nicotine as a drug, President Clinton and FDA Administrator Dr. David Kessler have a single purpose: to do everything possible to keep tobacco products out of the hands of children. This proposal does not target adult smokers, nor does it call for prohibition or a ban on all tobacco products.

TAKING UP THE HABIT DURING CHILDHOOD

Virtually all smokers begin to smoke during childhood, and if we can get our kids to age 18 without smoking, there is a good chance they will never take up the habit. More than 3 million American adolescents smoke, and some 3,000 take up the habit every day. Moreover, 82 percent of adults who ever smoked started before age 18, and more than half had become addicted by that age. Most teenagers who smoke, in fact, have made at least one unsuccessful attempt to quit.

There is really very little debate about the hazards of smoking. In fact, tobacco is the only legal product sold that, when used exactly as directed, will cause harm to the user as soon as such use begins. Kids who smoke get sore throats and develop recurrent coughs, and a lifetime of tobacco use increases one's odds of getting chronic lung disease, emphysema, and cancer.

Sadly, many children begin to smoke just to be a little rebellious or cool or macho or independent, only to discover all too quickly that they have become addicted to nicotine. And despite the tobacco industry's claims to the contrary, a mountain of evidence supports the fact that nicotine is probably the most physically addicting substance available.

AMERICANS FAVOR REGULATION

Regulation of substances is something we have come to expect from our government. We count on the FDA to make sure the foods we eat are healthy, the cosmetics we use are safe, and the medications we take are efficacious and free of dangerous side effects. Studies, including one completed recently for the Coalition on Smoking and Health, repeatedly show that Americans favor regulation of tobacco products by the FDA. Various surveys indicate that between two-thirds and three-fourths of adults believe that the agency should see to it that use is restricted to adults.

Nicotine is regulated when supplied as a patch or in gum used for smoking cessation, so that the consistency of the product can be controlled. The tobacco industry itself admits that the main purpose of a cigarette is to deliver nicotine (so the user gradually but inexorably becomes addicted), so why not regulate nicotine-delivery devices as carefully as the FDA regulates the other forms of the drug?

The FDA has chosen a careful route in its attempt to make a dent in youth smoking. It has gone to great lengths not to disturb present adult smokers. The concept of total prohibition is not mentioned in the current proposal, nor has it been a serious topic of discussion at any level. Rather, the FDA proposes to go after the tobacco industry at the promotional and retail level to force it to assume more responsibility in not promoting tobacco products to children. The proposed regulations are cautious, solid, and worthwhile and may go a long way toward convincing young people that, despite Joe Camel, Virginia Slims, and the Marlboro man touting illusions of popularity, happiness, and athleticism, smoking makes one nothing more than a smoker.

THE FDA'S PROPOSAL

Let's take a careful look at exactly what the FDA proposes, for there has been so much hysteria that many have lost sight of the fact that the intent is fairly narrow. The proposed rule would allow the sale of tobacco products only to persons over the age of 18 and would prohibit any distribution system that did not feature eye-to-eye contact between seller and purchaser. Gone would be vending machines favored by underage buyers, and mail sampling and giveaways would end. This regulation would really do nothing more than formalize a law that is already on the books—namely, no sales to children.

Sales of single cigarettes and small (cheaper) packs would also be banned, as these methods of buying cigarettes are especially appealing to children. There is not much of an impact on adult smokers here, either, as most adult smokers have the money to purchase packs or cartons.

SMOKING TO BE "KOOL"

Promotion of cigarettes has been especially targeted by this regulation. The image of smokers the cigarette companies have created has been brilliantly crafted. Industry psychologists have hit the nail on the head with their approach, for children begin to smoke for well-defined reasons. Teenagers rebel against their parents and society. They are into risk taking and staunch independence. They want to be perceived as trendsetters and "cool" and part of the "in" crowd. Girls especially strive for the allure of slimness and sexiness.

Cigarette advertisements turn cigarettes into symbols, linking smoking to success, peer group acceptance, sophistication, and a healthy, vibrant life-style. Thus, the Marlboro man is portrayed as rugged and independent. Joe Camel is totally "cool" and only hangs out with others of equal stature. Virginia Slims and Misty models are invariably sexy and skinny and oozing charm and polish. Newports are for breezy, fun-loving people, and certainly Kools are only for the truly "kool."

Reprinted by permission of Mike Luckovich and Creators Syndicate.

The statistics clearly show what any junior high school kid can tell us. The three most heavily advertised brands, Marlboro, Camel, and Newport, garner some 86 percent of the pediatric smokers' purchases, compared to their overall 35 percent market share. Within the youth market, Camel's share alone skyrocketed from 3 percent to 13 percent as a result of Joe Camel's fine work. Why should the industry be allowed to throw its millions of dollars around, creating the impression among our children that smoking is safe, awesome, and glamorous?

LIMITS ON ADVERTISING

The FDA proposes to limit advertising aimed at children in several specific ways. Billboards would not be permitted near schools and playgrounds. Print advertisements that reach a significant audience of young people would be restricted to black and white to eliminate the striking images to which children have been exposed. Sponsorship of sporting events such as auto races and tennis tournaments by specific brands would be prohibited, though the corporations themselves could continue to sponsor in their own name.

The distribution of premiums and brand-identified products such as clothing, luggage, and sporting gear would be prohibited, as these items clearly appeal most to the youth market. Finally the tobacco companies would have to establish and fund a national educational campaign to help reduce youth smoking by providing factual information to counter their products' appeal to children.

Why is the industry so upset at the proposed regulation? Quite simply, the tobacco industry knows that adults don't take up cigarette smoking. If it is to replace the 3,000 to 4,000 adults who die each day from tobacco-related illness, it must get children to take up the habit. Furthermore, the industry knows from the psychological profile that youth is very susceptible to the influences of image advertising and product association; it fears that if it can't get its message to kids, its sales will plummet.

It is critical to realize that the proposed FDA regulations in no way affect legitimate tobacco use or availability for adults. Advertisers can still easily and effectively get their message to the audience that can legitimately purchase their products. No attempt is made to affect the smoking patterns of adults. Given the dreadful health consequences associated with a lifetime of tobacco use, it is fair and in the public interest to do everything possible to restrict youth access to these products.

> "The evidence is [weak] that
> government restrictions on tobacco
> advertising reduce tobacco use."

INCREASED REGULATION OF TOBACCO PRODUCTS WOULD NOT REDUCE TEENAGE SMOKING

Dwight R. Lee

In recent years, federal, state, and local governments have attempted to reduce teen smoking with increased regulations of tobacco products. State governments have experimented with hikes in cigarette taxes, while the federal government has instituted regulations that restrict the advertising of tobacco products. Dwight R. Lee contends in the following viewpoint that neither measure will significantly reduce smoking among teenagers. He claims that high taxes on cigarettes only result in rampant cigarette smuggling, whereby minors have more, not less, access to cigarettes. Furthermore, smoking advertisements—both positive and negative—have little impact on whether teens decide to smoke. Lee is Ramsey Professor of Economics at the University of Georgia, Athens, and an adjunct fellow at the Center for the Study of American Business at Washington University in St. Louis, Missouri.

As you read, consider the following questions:

1. Why does the tobacco industry spend so much money on advertising, in the author's view?
2. According to Lee, why are the studies conducted on Joe Camel's impact on children inconclusive?

Reprinted from Dwight R. Lee, "The Government's Crusade Against Tobacco: Can It Ultimately Succeed?" *USA Today* magazine, May 1998, by permission of the Society for the Advancement of Education.

Federal, state, and local governments are crusading against tobacco. The charge is being led at the federal level by the Food and Drug Administration (FDA), with its restrictions on cigarette advertising. At the state level, 40 attorneys general have sued the tobacco industry for reimbursement for Medicaid expenses. State excise taxes have been increased on cigarettes, with much of the revenue earmarked for a host of anti-smoking mass media campaigns. This crusade led to a historic agreement whereby the tobacco industry would pay more than $360,000,000,000 over 25 years to reimburse states and fund anti-smoking media campaigns, among other things. Cigarette advertising would be further restricted, with no ads at sporting events, billboard ads, or pictures of humans or cartoons within those ads.

Will this crusade reduce smoking, particularly among teenagers? Probably not. Despite the claims of organizations that receive funding from tobacco tax revenues, punishing and preaching have not been, and are unlikely to be, significant factors influencing smoking rates, especially among teens. The evidence is even weaker that government restrictions on tobacco advertising reduce tobacco use.

Like most goods, the quantity of cigarettes demanded is related inversely to price. Increasing the price of cigarettes with excise taxes reduces the amount sold.

States that significantly have raised their excise tax on cigarettes have reported large reductions in cigarette sales. For example, New York and California have imposed sharp excise tax increases on cigarettes since 1988, and both report large declines in sales: 31% in New York and 28% in California. Similarly, Michigan's sales dropped 30% the year following a raise in taxes. Such evidence seems to support the argument that raising taxes is an effective way to reduce smoking. A closer look, however, shows that this is not the case.

RAISING CIGARETTE TAXES DOES NOT REDUCE SMOKING

When a state hikes its cigarette tax, the price of cigarettes taxed within its borders goes up. There also is an increase in the sale of cigarettes brought in from other states or jurisdictions with lower taxes. Some of these cross-border sales are the result of people bringing in small quantities of cigarettes after visits to nearby low-tax states, Indian reservations, and/or military bases where state taxes don't apply. Much of the cross-border traffic in cigarettes, though, is supplied by organized smuggling.

Michigan, for instance, has suffered from a smuggling epidemic since it raised the cigarette excise tax to 75 cents from 25 cents per pack in 1994. *The Detroit Free Press*, in a front-page article entitled "Smugglers Win," revealed pervasive smuggling networks in Michigan. According to the article, "Michigan's higher tobacco tax has spawned rampant cigarette smuggling that's siphoned millions of tax dollars from the state treasury, while lighting up huge profits for traffickers."

So, while legal cigarette sales in Michigan dropped by 30% from July 1, 1994, to June 30, 1995, this was not accompanied by a decline in smokers in the state. In fact, smoking rose in Michigan from 25.2 to 25.7% from 1993 to 1995, according to a survey by the Centers for Disease Control. Not surprisingly, while Michigan cigarette sales were dropping, those in low-tax states within a day's drive increased significantly. For example, in the year after the Michigan tax hike, sales rose 12% in North Carolina, 8.5% in Indiana, 7.5% in Tennessee, six percent in Kentucky and Missouri, and 4.5% in Ohio and Virginia.

Maryland raised its cigarette tax by 20 cents per pack in 1992 and, in the following year, sales of cigarettes taxed in that state fell by 10%. Yet, as in Michigan, the percentage of smokers in Maryland went up from 20.4 to 21.2% from 1993 to 1995. Obviously, the growth in cigarette sales in the low-tax states did not reflect large increases in smoking there. Rather, most of the rise in cigarettes sold in the low-tax states was to supply smokers in the high-tax states.

Similarly, the evidence from the large cigarette-excise tax hike in California provides little reason to believe that smoking significantly is reduced by state taxes. In 1988, it increased the state excise tax from 10 to 35 cents per pack. As could have been predicted, given the size of the California market and its proximity to low-taxed cigarettes in Mexico, Indian reservations, and military bases, contraband cigarettes began flooding into the state. It has been estimated that from 17.2 to 23% of the cigarettes sold in California come from contraband sales, with a major source being cigarettes exported to Mexico and then smuggled back into the U.S. This clearly suggests that the 28% decline in legal cigarette sales in California provides an unreliable measure of any reduction in smoking due to the tax hike. Interestingly, if contraband cigarettes make up just 13–14% of the California market, smoking there has not declined since the tax increase by any more than the nationwide average over the same period.

THE EXAMPLE OF CANADA

The experience of Canada is instructive as well. It widely was reported that smuggled cigarettes made up 30–50% of the Canadian market. Taxable cigarette sales nose-dived as taxes rose during the mid 1980s and early 1990s. At the same time, massive cigarette smuggling was making up for the apparent decline in smoking, as measured by legal, or tax-reported, Canadian sales. In the end, when all the cigarettes were counted, the Canadian smoking rate fell no more than in the U.S. during the same period.

Canada reduced its cigarette tax in 1994 by a substantial amount, as much as $22 per carton in some provinces, to stem a smuggling epidemic. It cut the tax rate not only because smuggling greatly was reducing the sale of taxable cigarettes, but because of concern over youth smoking. Contrary to the usual argument, many Canadian officials concluded that high taxes made it more difficult to control teenagers' access to cigarettes. To explain the tax cut, Canadian Health Minister Diane Marleau said, "It will end the smuggling trade and [force] children to rely on regular stores for their cigarettes, where they will be forbidden from buying them until they are 19."

State governments can raise the price of legally taxed cigarettes, but can do little to increase the price smokers pay for cigarettes unless they are willing to divert far more police resources from protecting the public against traditional crimes and into smuggling control than they seem willing to do. Hiking cigarette excise taxes is not a very effective way to reduce smoking.

ANTI-TOBACCO MEDIA CAMPAIGNS

What about preaching the "evils" of smoking through media campaigns funded by the revenue from high cigarette taxes? It appears that preaching is even less effective than taxation. Expensive media campaigns seem to have no long-run effect on tobacco use. At best, the evidence suggests that they are just one of many factors that influence decisions to smoke and that any influence they might have is short-lived.

Anti-tobacco ads that emphasize the health effects of smoking are particularly unsuccessful. Commenting on this ineffectiveness, Lisa Unsworth, executive vice president at the ad agency Houston Effler Herstek Favat (which has created anti-tobacco ads in Massachusetts), points out that "Kids think they will live forever. Talking about a disease that you may get when you're 50 or 60 isn't a compelling motivator." While there may be some truth in this comment, it is more likely that teens are not discouraged from smoking by health claims because they already have an exaggerated impression of the health risks of smoking.

Few things have been so widely disseminated and accepted as the evidence that smoking is harmful to your health. Research by Kip Viscusi, an economist at Harvard University, shows that people consistently overestimate the risks of smoking. In particular, Viscusi finds that teenagers believe smoking is a greater health hazard than indicated by the Surgeon General's reports and have a more exaggerated perception of the risks than adults do. Anti-smoking ads that emphasize health concerns simply do not provide teens with any new information. Therefore, it is not surprising that these ads have no long-run influence on their smoking behavior.

It is not that all anti-tobacco ads are ineffective or that no teenagers will stop smoking after being exposed to an anti-tobacco media campaign. Some evidence indicates that a number do stop smoking in response to certain types of ads. The important issue is the long-run influence of anti-tobacco ads, and here, the evidence for the effectiveness of these ads is very weak. Many teens experiment with smoking, but most quit, the majority for a wide range of reasons that have nothing to do with such advertising. An anti-tobacco media campaign marginally may affect the timing of a person's decision to quit, but there is no evidence that it affects the ultimate decision to do so.

POURING MONEY INTO INEFFECTIVE ADS

The objective of anti-tobacco ads targeted at teens is laudable. No responsible person favors youths smoking, which explains why laws against selling cigarettes to anyone under 18 long have existed in every state and the District of Columbia. No case can be made, though, for pouring resources into anti-tobacco ads if they are ineffective, no matter how laudable the objective.

Of course, those receiving money to prepare anti-tobacco media campaigns can be expected either to deny that their ads are ineffective or to argue that more money is needed to make them effective. In the still unratified agreement between the cigarette industry and government whereby the industry will pay over $360,000,000,000 in return for some degree of immunity against lawsuits, one report predicts that "about $500,000,000 would go toward anti-smoking education projects."

The claim is that anti-smoking campaigns must continue and expand to offset the large amount of money that the cigarette industry is spending on ads to encourage smoking. However, there is no credible evidence that anti-tobacco media campaigns have any long-run effect on smoking or that cigarette advertising does anything to encourage people to begin smoking.

Why would the tobacco industry spend so much on advertising if it is ineffective? Each company hopes to profit by convincing customers to use its brands rather than those of another manufacturer. Of course, if advertising does nothing to increase total consumption, all companies would be better off collectively if no one did so. The problem is in enforcing a general agreement not to advertise.

Bruce Beattie. Reprinted by permission of Copley News Service.

For each corporation, the best thing to do is advertise no matter what other companies in the industry are expected to do. Advertising will help a company increase market share if others do not advertise and will help avoid a decrease in market share if they do. For comparison's sake, advertising surely does nothing to raise the public's awareness of, or desire for, the convenience of automobile transportation. Car advertising can be explained entirely in terms of each auto company's desire to get consumers to purchase one of its models instead of a car from a competing manufacturer.

The teenage smoking rate in Finland was decreasing before 1978, the year the Finnish government imposed a nationwide ban on advertising tobacco products. After the ban, it began going up. A similar reversal in the teenage smoking rate occurred in Sweden after it imposed tight restrictions on tobacco advertising in 1979. There has been a ban on all tobacco advertising in Norway since 1975, with no noticeable effect on smoking and with the teenage smoking rate far higher than that experienced in countries with little, if any, restrictions on such advertising. In 1992, Australia imposed a ban on cigarette advertising, and smoking rates among adolescents rose.

This counterproductive response to advertising bans should not be surprising given the tendency of young people to rebel against what they see as restrictions on their independence. Adult disapproval of an activity often contributes to its popularity among the young. Turning smoking into a "forbidden fruit" easily can have the effect of increasing teenage smoking.

JOE CAMEL'S IMPACT

Yet, the media constantly are reporting claims that smoking in general, and youth smoking in particular, could be reduced significantly if only the government would impose additional restrictions on tobacco advertising. Most notable are the stories of studies indicating that the Joe Camel ads, before the R.J. Reynolds Tobacco Co. pulled them, enticed a large number of young people to smoke. It is true that the ads successfully boosted the market share of Camel cigarettes, but increasing the market share of one brand is not the same as increasing the number of young smokers or smokers of any age.

The study that attracted so much media attention found that 51.1% of the sampled three- to six-year-old children recognized the Camel cigarette cartoon character and that 91% of the six-year-olds correctly matched Joe Camel to cigarettes. It does not follow that recognizing Joe Camel makes an adult want to run out and smoke a cigarette or, even more implausibly, programs a four-year-old to want to start smoking Camel cigarettes 10 years later. Paul Fischer and his colleagues would not have had an interesting paper if all they said was that children are good at remembering cartoon characters. So they also claimed "that brand awareness created in childhood can be the basis for product preference later in life." This is based on the assumption that frequent exposure not only increases recognition of a product's trade character, but leads to a favorable attitude toward it. Yet, research has shown that there is not a necessary connection between repeated exposure to an advertisement, recognizing the ad, and a favorable attitude toward the product.

In another study, Richard Mizerski investigated not just the ability of children to recognize Joe Camel and associate this cartoon character with cigarettes, but the connection between such recognition and the attitude of the children toward cigarettes. He found that greater recognition of Joe Camel is associated with an increased dislike of cigarettes. According to Mizerski, "Comparing the recognition of Joe Camel and the liking of cigarettes across each age group illuminates the strong negative relationship between the two." Furthermore, he states, "With Joe Camel, I found no link between recognizing their associated products and the measure used to predict future use."

RESEARCH ON CIGARETTE ADVERTISING IS INCONCLUSIVE

Two additional studies, conveniently announced as the FDA was pushing for more control over tobacco advertising, claim to show that cigarette advertising significantly increases the likelihood adolescents will start smoking. Based on telephone interviews with 3,536 California adolescents who said they never had smoked, Nicola Evans and her colleagues found, after trying to take peer pressure into consideration, that those rated as receptive to cigarette advertising were two to four times more likely to be in the group classified as susceptible to smoking than those rated as unreceptive to advertising. In the second, John Pierce and his colleagues found a correlation between increased smoking among 14- to 17-year-olds and each of the four major advertising drives since the late 1800s. Pierce maintains that his studies establish advertising as a major influence, even more so than peer pressure, on the rate of teenage smoking.

Even those who see Evans' and Pierce's work as justifying action against cigarette advertising point out that their studies have failed to distinguish cause and effect and therefore are inconclusive. It is just as likely that a predisposition to smoking causes teens to be more receptive to cigarette advertising than the opposite. Or some third factor not considered by Evans could be the major influence behind both receptivity to cigarette advertising and susceptibility to smoking.

Pierce argues that the advertising caused the rise in teenage smoking. Yet, nothing in his study suggests that this is more likely than the growth in teenage smoking (and smoking in general) motivating cigarette companies to increase their advertising in an effort to expand market share. If the advertising campaigns caused the increase in smoking, why only four drives and why did they occur when they did? Why didn't the cigarette companies continue the high level of advertising associated with the drives if they were so effective at causing more people to smoke? Or does Pierce believe that the cigarette companies decided that they didn't want the increased business and profits that would have resulted from the additional advertising?

Unfazed by these flaws, the authors of these studies are eager to draw policy conclusions from their research they can not support. According to Pierce, "If something appears dangerous, we pull it. The prudent public health policy would be to pull [cigarette] marketing until they can prove it does no harm." This is a strange comment for a scientist to make. As Pierce surely is aware, it is impossible to prove any empirical proposition; all we can do is accept or reject such propositions at specified levels of confidence, always recognizing that we may be mistaken. Pierce is pushing a political agenda, not making a scientific defense of his studies. He also is recommending a policy that no sane person would want to generalize to the advertising of all products that some groups believe are harmful.

PERIODICAL BIBLIOGRAPHY

The following articles have been selected to supplement the diverse views presented in this chapter. Addresses are provided for periodicals not indexed in the *Readers' Guide to Periodical Literature*, the *Alternative Press Index*, the *Social Sciences Index*, or the *Index to Legal Periodicals and Books*.

D.T. Armentano — "Teen Smoking: The New Prohibition," *Freeman*, January 1997. Available from the Foundation for Economic Education, 30 S. Broadway, Irvington-on-Hudson, NY 10533.

Andrew M. Budai — "Make Way for the Tobacco Cops and Beware," *Insight*, November 4, 1996. Available from 3600 New York Ave. NE, Washington, DC 20002.

Joseph A. Califano Jr. — "Fictions and Facts About Drug Legalization," *America*, March 16, 1996.

William J. Chambliss — "Another Lost War: The Costs and Consequences of Drug Prohibition," *Social Justice*, Summer 1995.

Samuel Francis — "War on Smoking: Excuse for Bigger Government," *Conservative Chronicle*, September 11, 1996. Available from PO Box 11297, Des Moines, IA 50340.

Mike Males — "Gotta Match?" *In These Times*, August 5, 1996.

David Nyhan — "Facing the Facts in the War on Drugs," *Liberal Opinion*, November 20, 1995. Available from PO Box 468, Vinton, IA 52349.

Kathleen M. Paralusz — "Ashes to Ashes: Why FDA Regulation of Tobacco Advertising May Mark the End of the Road for the Marlboro Man," *American Journal of Law & Medicine*, vol. 24, no. 1, 1998.

Michael Pertschuk — "Fight Smoke with Fire: Why the White House Should Embrace Efforts to Stop the Tobacco Industry from Targeting Kids," *American Prospect*, Summer 1995.

A.M. Rosenthal — "Those Who Would Legalize Drugs Play the Cruelest Hoax," *New York Times*, January 4, 1995.

Sally L. Satel — "For Addicts, Force Is the Best Medicine," *Wall Street Journal*, January 6, 1998.

FOR FURTHER DISCUSSION

CHAPTER 1

1. Eric Niiler contends that addiction is a brain disease over which addicts have little control. Sally L. Satel, on the other hand, objects to the notion that addicts are not responsible for their own behavior. Based on these authors' arguments, do you think that addiction is a disease, as Niiler states, or a behavioral condition, as Satel maintains? Explain your answer.

2. Kevin J. Volpe argues that marijuana use leads to the use of highly addictive drugs such as cocaine. John Morgan and Lynn Zimmer disagree. How do the authors differ in their views on whether marijuana is dangerous? What evidence can you find that Volpe is opposed to marijuana use? What evidence can you find that Morgan and Zimmer do not oppose it?

3. According to the Hazelden Foundation, young people who drink have an increased risk of developing problems with alcohol later in life. In contrast, Stanton Peele believes that children who are exposed to alcohol early in life have a decreased risk of becoming alcoholics. Whose argument do you find more persuasive? Why?

CHAPTER 2

1. Join Together provides statistics that demonstrate a rise in teenage drug abuse. Sharon Cargo, arguing the opposite view, also cites statistics. Whose statistics do you find more convincing and why?

2. William Everett Bailey maintains that nicotine is a highly addictive substance. Lauren A. Colby questions whether nicotine is addictive at all. What evidence do the authors supply to support their views? Based on this evidence, whose argument is more persuasive and why?

3. Bernard P. Horn contends that compulsive gambling is a serious problem. Dick Boland disagrees. How are their views influenced by their differing opinions about whether gambling is an authentic addiction?

4. How do W. Waldo and Stanton Peele differ in their views on the nature of alcoholism? What evidence do they use to back up their opinions? Do you accept Waldo's assertion that alcoholism is a disease over which alcoholics have no control, or do you agree with Peele's belief that alcoholism is a choice? Explain your answer.

CHAPTER 3

1. The National Institute on Drug Abuse (NIDA) contends that the more treatment recovering addicts receive, the less likely they are to relapse. Anita Dubey, in contrast, argues that addicts can recover without treatment if they possess social support systems. Based on the evidence these authors provide, whose argument do you find more persuasive and why?

2. Controlled drinking has been proposed as an alternative to traditional alcoholism treatment programs that stress abstinence. According to Nancy Shute and Laura Tangley, some problem drinkers can learn to moderate their consumption of alcohol. The Hazelden Foundation and James E. Royce, on the other hand, believe that problem drinkers can never drink responsibly. How do these groups' different views on the definition of alcoholism influence their beliefs about the feasibility of controlled drinking?

3. One of the most controversial approaches to heroin addiction is the proposal to supply addicts with legal heroin. Proponents of this approach, including Ethan Nadelmann, argue that supplying addicts with heroin prevents the societal costs of addiction such as health care expenses, the spread of AIDS, and crime. Robert Maginnis and other opponents of heroin maintenance contend that the only goal of drug treatment programs should be abstinence. How do these two authors differ in their opinion on whether a drug-free society is possible? Whose view do you find more convincing and why?

CHAPTER 4

1. Randy E. Barnett argues that legalizing drugs would benefit both addicts and society. Erich Goode, on the other hand, believes that if illegal drugs were made legal, more people would use and become addicted to drugs. Based on these authors' arguments, what are the advantages and disadvantages of drug legalization?

2. According to Public Agenda, the government must vigorously enforce drug laws and impose strict penalties on drug traffickers, dealers, and users. Is the author's plea for "zero tolerance" for illegal drugs realistic? Based on what you have read in this book, will tough law enforcement measures deter people from using drugs? Why or why not?

3. Richard B. Heyman asserts that restrictions on tobacco advertising will result in less teen smoking. Dwight R. Lee disputes the notion that advertising encourages teenagers to smoke. What evidence do the authors provide to support their views? Whose evidence do you find more convincing and why?

ORGANIZATIONS TO CONTACT

The editors have compiled the following list of organizations concerned with the issues debated in this book. The descriptions are derived from materials provided by the organizations. All have publications or information available for interested readers. The list was compiled on the date of publication of the present volume; the information provided here may change. Be aware that many organizations take several weeks or longer to respond to inquiries, so allow as much time as possible.

Addiction Resource Guide
PO Box 8612, Tarrytown, NY 10591
(914) 725-5151 • fax: (914) 631-8077
e-mail: pbwaldman@aol.com
website: http://www.hubplace.com/addictions
The Addiction Resource Guide is a comprehensive on-line directory of addiction treatment facilities, programs, and resources. The Inpatient Treatment Facility directory provides in-depth profiles of treatment facilities and is indexed by name, location, and special populations served. The site recently expanded to include eating disorders and other non-chemical addictions. The site has community resources, information on how to navigate the treatment process, resources for professionals, and a glossary of addiction-related terms.

Alcoholics Anonymous (AA)
General Service Office
PO Box 459, New York, NY 10163
(212) 870-3400 • fax: (212) 870-3003
website: http://www.alcoholics-anonymous.org
Alcoholics Anonymous is a worldwide fellowship of sober alcoholics whose recovery is based on a twelve-step program. AA's main purpose is to help alcoholics remain sober and carry their message to alcoholics who still suffer and seek help. It publishes a catalog of literature concerning the organization as well as several pamphlets, including *Young People and AA* and *A Message to Teenagers: How to Tell When Drinking Is Becoming a Problem*.

Canadian Foundation on Compulsive Gambling (CFCG)
505 Consumers Rd., Suite 801, Willowdale, ON M2J 4V8, CANADA
(416) 499-9800 • fax: (416) 499-8260
e-mail: cfcg@interlog.com • website: http://www.cfcg.on.ca
CFCG conducts research into compulsive gambling and provides summaries of Ontario residents' attitudes and behavior regarding gambling. It publishes pamphlets on compulsive and teen gambling and has produced a high school curriculum and educational video about problem gambling.

Fight Ordinances & Restrictions to Control & Eliminate Smoking (FORCES)
PO Box 591257, San Francisco, CA 94159
(415) 824-4716 • fax: (415) 206-0991
e-mail: info@forces.org • website: http://www.forces.org
Founded in 1995, FORCES is an international not-for-profit organization that opposes smoking bans and misinformation about second-hand smoke. It is dedicated to the protection and restoration of the civil and human rights of smokers. Its website features on-line articles and essays as well as links to studies, research reports, membership information, and other Internet resources.

Moderation Management (MM)
PO Box 1752, Woodinville, WA 98072
(425) 844-8228
e-mail: mm@moderation.org • website: http://moderation.org
Moderation Management is a recovery program and national support group for people who have made the decision to reduce their drinking and make other positive lifestyle changes. MM empowers individuals to accept personal responsibility for choosing and maintaining their own recovery path, whether moderation or abstinence. It offers the book *Moderate Drinking: The Moderation Management Guide for People Who Want to Reduce Their Drinking* as well as suggested reading material, books, pamphlets, and guidelines regarding drinking in moderation.

National Center on Addiction and Substance Abuse (CASA)
Columbia University
152 W. 57th St., New York, NY 10019
(212) 841-5200 • fax: (212) 956-8020
website: http://www.casacolumbia.org
The National Center on Addiction and Substance Abuse at Columbia University brings together the professional disciplines needed to study and combat all types of substance abuse. CASA works to inform Americans of the economic and social costs of substance abuse; assess prevention, treatment, and law enforcement programs; and remove the stigma of substance abuse. Publications include *Substance Abuse and the American Woman* and *Legalization: Panacea or Pandora's Box*.

National Coalition Against Legalized Gambling (NCALG)
110 Maryland Ave. NE, Washington, DC 20002
(800) 664-2680
e-mail: ncalg@ncalg.org • website: http://www.ncalg.org
NCALG is an anti-gambling organization that seeks to educate the public, policy makers, and media about the social and economic costs of gambling. Publications include a quarterly newsletter and numerous on-line fact sheets and news articles.

National Institute on Drug Abuse (NIDA)
U.S. Department of Health and Human Services
5600 Fishers Ln., Rockville, MD 20857
(301) 443-6245
e-mail: information@nida.nih.gov
website: http://www.nida.nih.gov

NIDA conducts research on drug abuse—including the yearly Monitoring the Future survey—in order to improve addiction prevention, treatment, and policy efforts. It publishes the bimonthly NIDA Notes newsletter, periodic NIDA Capsules fact sheets, and a catalog of research reports and public education materials such as Marijuana: Facts for Teens.

National Organization for the Reform of Marijuana Laws (NORML)
1001 Connecticut Ave. NW, Suite 710, Washington, DC 20036
(202) 483-5500 • fax: (202) 483-0057
e-mail: norml@norml.org • website: http://www.norml.org

NORML was founded in 1970 and has been a principal advocate for legalizing marijuana ever since. The organization provides information to the national media on marijuana-related stories, lobbies state and federal legislators to permit the medical use of marijuana, and serves as the umbrella group for a national network of activists committed to ending marijuana prohibition. NORML produces a free newsletter with news updates on marijuana law reform and medical uses of marijuana and offers legal help for individuals charged with marijuana offenses.

RAND
1700 Main St., PO Box 2138, Santa Monica, CA 90407-2138
(310) 393-0411 • fax: (310) 393-4818
website: http://www.rand.org

RAND is a nonprofit institution that works to improve domestic and foreign policy and decision-making through research and analysis. Its drug policy research center offers numerous publications on topics ranging from drug policy and trends to prevention and treatment. All can be ordered directly from its website.

Secular Organizations for Sobriety (SOS)
5521 Grosvenor Blvd., Los Angeles, CA 90066
(310) 821-8430 • fax: (310) 821-2610
e-mail: sosla@loop.com • website: http://www.unhooked.com

SOS is an alternative recovery method for alcoholics or drug addicts who are uncomfortable with the spiritual content of twelve-step programs. SOS takes a secular approach to recovery and maintains that sobriety is a separate issue from religion or spirituality. Its publications include the books How to Stay Sober: Recovery Without Religion and Unhooked: Staying Sober and Drug Free as well as the quarterly SOS National Newsletter.

BIBLIOGRAPHY OF BOOKS

William Everett Bailey	*The Invisible Drug.* Cincinnati: Mosaic, 1996.
Dan Baum	*Smoke and Mirrors: The War on Drugs and the Politics of Failure.* Boston: Little, Brown, 1996.
Henri Begleiter and Benjamin Kissin	*The Genetics of Alcoholism.* New York: Oxford University Press, 1995.
Janet Bringham	*Dying to Quit: Why We Smoke and How We Stop.* Washington, DC: Joseph Henry Press, 1998.
Karen Casey	*If Only I Could Quit: Recovering from Nicotine Addiction.* Center City, MN: Hazelden, 1995.
Alan Dean	*Chaos and Intoxication: Complexity and Adaptation in the Structure of Human Nature.* New York: Routledge 1997.
Edward F. Dolan	*Teenagers and Compulsive Gambling.* Danbury, CT: Franklin Watts, 1994.
Scott Dowling, ed.	*The Psychology and Treatment of Addictive Behavior.* Madison, CT: International Universities Press, 1995.
William R. Eadington and Judy A. Cornelius, eds.	*Gambling Behavior and Problem Gambling.* Reno: University of Nevada Press, 1993.
Ralph H. Earle and Marcus R. Earle	*Sex Addiction: Case Studies and Management.* New York: Brunner/Mazel, 1995.
Griffith Edwards and Malcolm H. Lader	*Addiction: Processes of Change.* New York: Oxford University Press, 1994.
Patricia G. Erickson et al., eds.	*Harm Reduction: A New Direction for Drug Policies and Programs.* Toronto, Canada: University of Toronto Press, 1997.
Vince Fox	*Addiction, Change and Choice: The New View of Alcoholism.* Tucson: Sharp Press, 1995.
Lawrence S. Friedman, ed.	*Source Book of Substance Abuse and Addiction.* Baltimore: Williams & Wilkins, 1996.
Robert Goodman	*The Luck Business: The Devastating Consequences and Broken Promises of America's Gambling Explosion.* New York: Free Press, 1995.
Jill Jonnes	*Hep-Cats, Narcs, and Pipe Dreams: A History of America's Romance with Illegal Drugs.* New York: Scribner, 1996.
Audrey Kishline	*Moderate Drinking: The Moderation Management Guide for People Who Want to Reduce Their Drinking.* New York: Crown Trade Paperbacks, 1996.

Richard Klein

Cigarettes Are Sublime. Durham, NC: Duke University Press, 1993.

Susan S. Lang and
Beth H. Marks

Teens and Tobacco: A Fatal Attraction. New York: Twenty First Century Books, 1996.

James R. Milam and
Katherine Ketcham

Under the Influence: A Guide to the Myths and Realities of Alcoholism. Seattle: Madrona, 1981.

Gennaro Ottomanelli

Children and Addiction. Westport, CT: Praeger, 1995.

Stanton Peele

Diseasing of America: How We Allowed Recovery Zealots and the Treatment Industry to Convince Us We Are out of Control. New York: Lexington Books, 1995.

Stanton Peele

The Meaning of Addiction: An Unconventional View. San Francisco: Jossey Bass, 1998.

Stanton Peele and
Archie Brodsky

The Truth About Addiction and Recovery: The Life Process Program for Outgrowing Destructive Habits. New York: Simon & Schuster, 1991.

David A. Peters

The Probability of Addiction: Legal, Medical, and Social Implications. San Francisco: Austin & Winfield, 1997.

Marc Alan Schuckit

Educating Yourself About Alcohol and Drugs: A People's Primer. New York: Plenum Press, 1995.

Joseph Sora, ed.

Substance Abuse. New York: H.W. Wilson, 1997.

Paul B. Stares

Global Habit: The Drug Problem in a Borderless World. Washington, DC: Brookings Institution, 1996.

Jacob Sullum

For Your Own Good: The Anti-Smoking Crusade and the Tyranny of Public Health. New York: Free Press, 1998.

Jack Trimpey

Rational Recovery: The New Cure for Substance Addiction. New York: Simon & Schuster, 1996.

George E. Vaillant

The Natural History of Alcoholism. Cambridge, MA: Harvard University Press, 1983.

William L. White

Slaying the Dragon: The History of Addiction Treatment and Recovery in America. Bloomington, IL: Chestnut Health Systems, 1998.

Lynn Zimmer and
John P. Morgan

Marijuana Myths; Marijuana Facts: A Review of the Scientific Evidence. New York: Lindesmith Center, 1997.

FOOTNOTES FOR THE DANGERS OF ALCOHOL ARE EXAGGERATED

1. J.R. Milam and K. Ketcham, *Under the Influence: A Guide to the Myths and Realities of Alcoholism* (Bantam Books, 1983), 42.

2. J. Merry, "The 'loss of control' myth," *Lancet* 1(1966):1257–58; J. Langenbucher and P.E. Nathan, "The 'wet' alcoholic: One drink . . . then what?" in *Identifying and Measuring Alcoholic Personality Characteristics*, ed. W.M. Cox (Jossey-Bass, 1983).

3. G.A. Marlatt, B. Demming, and J.B. Reid, "Loss of control drinking in alcoholics: An experimental analogue," *Journal of Abnormal Psychology* 81(1973):223–41.

4. N.K. Mello and J.H. Mendelson, "A quantitative analysis of drinking patterns in alcoholics," *Archives of General Psychiatry* 25(1971):527–39.

5. G.A. Marlatt, "Alcohol, the magic elixir," in *Stress and Addiction*, eds. E. Gottheil et al. (Brunner/Mazel, 1987).

6. N.K. Mello and J.H. Mendelson, "Drinking patterns during work-contingent and non-contingent alcohol acquisition," *Psychosomatic Medicine* 34(1972):1116–21.

7. G. Bigelow, I.A. Liebson, and R. Griffiths, "Alcoholic drinking: Suppression by a brief time-out procedure," *Behavior Research and Therapy* 12(1974): 107–15; M. Cohen, I.A. Liebson, L.A. Faillace, and R.P. Allen, "Moderate drinking by chronic alcoholics: A schedule-dependent phenomenon," *Journal of Nervous and Mental Disorders*.

8. G.D. Talbott, in *The Courage to Change*, ed. D. Wholey (Houghton Mifflin, 1984), 19.

9. Cahalan and Room, *Problem Drinking*.

10. K.M. Fillmore, "Relationships between specific drinking problems in early adulthood and middle age," *Journal of Studies on Alcohol* 36(1975):892–907; M.T. Temple and K.M. Fillmore, "The variability of drinking patterns and problems among young men, age 16–31," *International Journal of Addiction* 20(1986):1595–1620.

11. S. Peele, "What can we expect from treatment of adolescent drug and alcohol abuse?" *Pediatrician* 14(1987):62–69.

12. E. Harburg, D.R. Davis, and R. Caplan, "Parent and offspring alcohol use," *Journal of Studies on Alcohol* 43(1982):497–516.

13. E. Harburg et al., "Familial transmission of alcohol use: II. Imitation and aversion to parent drinking (1960) by adult offspring (1977)," *Journal of Studies on Alcohol*, in press.

14. G. Elal-Lawrence, P.D. Slade, and M.E. Dewey, "Predictors of outcome type in treated problem drinkers," *Journal of Studies on Alcohol* 47(1986):41–47; M. Sanchez-Craig, D.A. Wilkinson, and K. Walker, "Theories and methods for secondary prevention of alcohol problems," in *Treatment and Prevention of Alcohol Problems*, ed. W.M. Cox (Academic Press, 1987).

15. P. Biernacki, *Pathways from Heroin Addiction: Recovery Without Treatment* (Temple University Press, 1986).

16. M.M. Gross, "Psychobiological contributions to the alcohol dependence syndrome" in *Alcohol Related Disabilities*, eds. G. Edwards et al. (World Health Organization, 1977), 121.

17. B.S. Tuchfeld, "Spontaneous remission in alcoholics," *Journal of Studies on Alcohol* 42(1981):626–41.

18. L.R.H. Drew, "Alcoholism as a self-limiting disease," *Quarterly Journal of Studies on Alcohol* 29(1968):956–67.

19. H.A. Mulford, "Rethinking the alcohol problem: A natural process model," *Journal of Drug Issues* 14(1984):38.

INDEX

abstinence, drug and alcohol
  is not a realistic goal, 41
  as traditional treatment for
    alcoholism, 94
acupuncture, 128–30
addiction
  as behavioral condition, 27
  definition of, 54, 59
  and free will, 25–27
  heroin, methadone is effective
    treatment for, 107–10
    con, 111–13
  is a disease, 17–23
    con, 24–27
  nicotine
    characteristics of, 55
    smoking causes, 53–57
      con, 58–60
  potential of substances, 18
  role of dopamine in, 19–20
advertising, of cigarettes, 167
  Joe Camel's impact, 175–76
  motives behind, 173–74
  proposed limits on, 168
  research on, is inconclusive, 176–77
AIDS
  and harm reduction approach, 117,
    124
alcohol
  abuse, dangers are exaggerated,
    74–78
  addictive nature of, 18
  attitudes in U.S. on, 95, 97
  blood concentration after drinks, 96
  vs. cocaine, link with violent crime,
    163
  health benefits of, 41
  problem drinking
    costs of, 94–95
    distinction between alcoholism and,
      95, 103, 104
  underage use of, increases risk of
    alcoholism, 35–38
    con, 39–42
  use among teenagers, 48, 51
Alcoholics Anonymous, 94
alcoholism
  alcoholic progression, myth of,
    76–77
  definition of, 71, 94
  as disease concept, 26, 97–98
  genetic factors, 12, 72–73

is a serious problem, 70–73
learning moderation can help,
  93–100
  con, 101–106
people outgrow, 77–78
prevalence of, 71–72
vs. problem drinking, 94, 103, 104
rates are overestimated, 77
self-cure of, 78, 90
underage drinking increases risk of,
  35–38
  con, 39–42
Alexander, Lamar, 30
Alman, Brian, 130
American Civil Liberties Union, 139
American Gaming Association, 69
American Journal of Public Health, 88
American Psychiatric Association
  on addiction, 54
  on compulsive gambling, 63
American Society of Addiction
  Medicine, 71
amphetamines
  addictive nature of, 18
anti-addiction drugs, 22–23
Apollonian approach to life
  vs. Dionysian approach, 145–46
Apostolides, Marianne, 123

Bailey, William Everett, 53
Bain, George, 45
Barnett, Randy E., 136
Beecher, Lyman, 97
Beilenson, Peter, 120, 121
Benedict, Ruth, 145
Between Politics and Reason (Goode), 144
Block, Marvin, 105
Boland, Dick, 67
bone growth
  effects of alcohol use on, 37
brain
  effects of heavy drug use on, 25
  effects of nicotine on, 56–57
  pleasure pathway in, 21

Cahalan, Don, 76
Califano, Joseph A., Jr., 150, 160
California v. Cabazon Band of Mission Indians,
  62
Cargo, Sharon, 49
Caron, Marc, 22
casinos